KABBALAH

The Way of the Jewish Mystic

KABBALAH

The Way of the Jewish Mystic

PERLE EPSTEIN

Foreword by Edward Hoffman

SHAMBHALA
Boston & London
1988

For Jerry, Colette, and Rav Kook

Shambhala Publications, Inc.
Horticultural Hall
300 Massachusetts Avenue
Boston, Massachusetts 02115
http://www.shambhala.com

12   11   10   9   8
Printed in the United States of America
♾ This edition is printed on acid-free paper that meets the American National Standards Institute Z39.48 Standard.
Distributed in the United States by Random House, Inc., and in Canada by Random House of Canada, Ltd

Library of Congress Cataloging-in-Publication Data
Epstein, Perle S.
    Kabbalah : the way of the Jewish mystic.
    Reprint. Originally published: Garden City, N.Y.:
Doubleday, 1978.
    Bibliography: p.
    1. Cabala—History.   2. Hasidism—History.
I. Title.
BM526.E67   1988   296.1′6   87-28833
ISBN 0-87773-438-0 (pbk.)

Grateful acknowledgment is given to the following for permission to reprint:
    Excerpts from *The Life and Works of Moses Hayyim Luzzatto* by Simon Ginzburg and used with the agreement of the reprint publisher, Greenwood Press, Inc.
    Excerpts from *Major Trends in Jewish Mysticism* by Gerschom G. Scholem. Copyright © 1946, 1954 by Schocken Books, Inc. Copyright renewed © 1974 by Schocken Books, Inc. Reprinted by permission of Schocken Books, Inc.
    Excerpts from *The Path of the Just* by M. C. Luzzatto, translated by Shraga Silverstein. Reprinted by permission of Feldheim Publishers, Jerusalem-New York.
    Excerpts from *Rabbi Nachman's Wisdom*, translated by Aryeh Kaplan. Copyright © 1973 by Aryeh Kaplan. Published privately; distributed by Hermon Press. Used by permission of the author.

CONTENTS

FOREWORD   *ix*

INTRODUCTION   *xiii*

I THE MYSTIC LIFE

CHAPTER 1. The Preparatory Phase: Cultivating Awe   2
*The Hidden Garden—Bahya ben Joseph Ibn Paquda:
"Know God with Your Heart"—Safed: The Jewish
Shangri-La—Moses Cordovero's "Thirteen Divine
Attributes"—The Tree of Life—Isaac Luria: The
"Lion" of Safed—Moses Luzzatto and His Circle—The
Secrets of Beth El*

CHAPTER 2. Love: The Journey to God   34
*Warnings to the Voyager—A Vision of the Absolute—
Rabbi Nehuniah ben Hakana: Approaching the
Throne of God—The Book of Light—Revealing the
Cosmic Body—The Female Aspect of God—Passion-
ate Seekers After God*

II KABBALISTIC PRACTICES

CHAPTER 3: The Path of Spheres   54
*Rabbi Simeon bar Yohai and the Zohar—King Solo-
mon's Breathing Exercise—Meditation on the Shema
—Abraham's Spiritual Journey—Binding of the
Spheres—Parallels to Taoist Meditation*

CHAPTER 4: The Path of Letters   73
*Abraham Abulafia: Master of Tzeruf (Letter Permu-
tation)—The Mystical Rabble Rouser—Enthusiasm—*

Contents

Meditation on the Name—Shefa: *The Divine Influx—Letters the Size of Mountains—Isaac of Akko: "Kill the Self for the Torah"—Later Reflections on* Tzeruf

CHAPTER 5: The Path of Ecstasy: Hasidism   107
The Baal Shem Tov: Human, Practical, and Wise—The Hasidic Method: Prayer—An Itinerant Preacher Becomes the Baal Shem Tov's Disciple—The Hasid's Journey Through the Unconscious—Three Giants—Rebbe Nachman's Conversations with God—Rebbe Shneur Zalman: The Intellectual Mystic—Subduing the Animal Self—Building the Perfect Shabbat—*Dov Baer of Lubavitch: The Ten Stages of Ecstasy*

III   DEVEKUTH: CLEAVING TO GOD

CHAPTER 6: The Way of God   142
Prophecy—Supernatural Guides—The Secret Diary of Joseph Caro—The Highest Vision

EPILOGUE: Personal Musings on a Future Kabbalah   158

GLOSSARY   164

BIBLIOGRAPHY   168

Author's Note

Special thanks to Rabbi Aryeh Kaplan, my translator, for his insightful interpretations of much convoluted material in both Hebrew and Aramaic. His personal involvement in Kabbalah has enriched my own work beyond the scope of mere translation.

Acknowledgments

Hebrew University Libraries, specifically Mr. Benjamin Richler of the Microfilm Division, Jerusalem, Israel.

Bodleian Library, Oxford, England.

Bibliothèque Nationale, Paris, France.

Jewish Theological Seminary Library, specifically Ms. Susan Winter and Mr. Micah Oppenheim, New York, New York.

Vatican Library, Vatican City.

Mr. Tovyah Lasdun of Feldheim Book Publishers, New York, New York.

Mr. Donald Weiser of Samuel Weiser Books, New York, New York.

Columbia University Library Manuscript Division, New York, New York.

British Museum, London, England.

Professor Jeremy Zwelling, Wesleyan University, Middletown, Connecticut.

Rabbi Alexandre Safran, University of Geneva, Geneva, Switzerland.

Professor Ruth Reichelberg, Bar Ilan University, Ramat Gan, Israel.

Ms. Alma Khayenko, Jerusalem, Israel.

Mr. Abraham Samet, Jerusalem, Israel.

Dr. Nili Livni, Hadassah Hospital, Jerusalem, Israel.

FOREWORD

It seems very fitting for me to introduce this reissue of *Kabbalah: The Way of the Jewish Mystic*—a seminal, exciting influence upon my own exploration of the Kabbalah. Amid the dark, confused sea of most books seeking to describe this exotic realm, I found Perle Epstein's a clear beacon lighting the way to comprehending what Jewish mysticism is all about. Her strong historical emphasis, direct quotations from sacred texts, and appropriate use of Hebrew terms all helped me enormously in my initial quest to make sense of a vast, frequently bewildering territory.

This book also confirmed my initial suspicion that the Kabbalah shares many intriguing features with other esoteric traditions. You will find, for example, that altered forms of breathing, special bodily postures, and complex visualizations are all quite germane to Jewish mysticism, and not only to Yoga or Taoism. With a strong ecumenical sensitivity, Dr. Epstein highlights these striking similarities of thought and practice throughout her work.

Writing when she did, in the mid-seventies, this was no easy task. Aside from Gershom Scholem's dry, scholarly narratives and Martin Buber's stylized renditions of early Hasidic tales, there was virtually nothing of true worth in the English language written on the subject. To one wishing to learn something meaningful about the Kabbalah, matters were disappointing indeed. Sure, you could find occultist accounts about the Kabbalah, but

Foreword

these were—and still are—of very questionable value, especially to the novice. As the sages have said, half-truths are sometimes more dangerous than lies, and such tomes are filled with inaccuracies and distortions.

Not so Perle Epstein's book. With a strong yeshiva background, I immediately found in her *Kabbalah* a real appreciation for Judaism—its age-old outlook and way of life. Unlike to many other works about its esoteric tradition, this one communicated an authentic Jewish spirit, and that appealed to me very much. It still does. She convincingly shows how the broad structure of Judaism has over the centuries provided a framework for individual, mystical expression: from contemplation of the Bible's secret teachings to ecstatic prayer and Hebrew alphabet meditative techniques. In a lucid manner, she shows that Kabbalists stand on the firm ground of ethics in all their activity: that climbing the heavenly ladder is always a patient, step-by-step journey toward the divine.

Yet it is really no surprise that Perle Epstein conveys this Jewish spirit so well. Growing up in New York City, she received a very substantial training in traditional Judaism—about as much as possible for any woman in those days. Perhaps equally important, her chief teacher for several adult years was Rabbi Aryeh Kaplan—a foremost interpreter and translator of classic Kabbalistic texts, whose death has been a great loss to us all. He spent countless hours with her, sharpening her sensitivity to the inherent subtleties of the sacred writings, and making personally available their English translation for the first time in history. The Kabbalah has always emphasized that we find the best teachers possible, and Dr. Epstein's book demonstrates that she followed this principle well.

Certainly, there has been a tremendous explosion of interest in Jewish mysticism since this book first appeared. There is fortunately much, much more now available in the way of cogent classes, workshops, and well-translated primary texts. Lively curiosity concerning Judaism's esoteric branch is steadily growing and is hardly limited to a few big cities in North America.

Foreword

Partly in response to my own pertinent books and presentations, I receive requests almost daily from men and women in out-of-the-way places who wish to connect more fully with Kabbalistic study and practice. All over the planet, people of all faiths and backgrounds are suddenly experiencing an intense attraction for this ancient path of knowledge. So read the last chapter of *Kabbalah: The Way of the Jewish Mystic* for its accurate picture of where things stood not too long ago, when Kabbalistic inquiry outside of the Hasidic communities was quite a lonely, solitary thing.

But the past decade of Kabbalistic exploration has not dimmed the relevance of Dr. Epstein's book. It remains an absorbing guide to the dazzling universe of Jewish mysticism, and enriches our understanding of this age-old tradition of wisdom and knowledge.

EDWARD HOFFMAN, PH.D.

INTRODUCTION

A thirteenth-century Jewish mystic was approached by a disciple who wished to learn the art of *hitbodedut,* or meditation.

"Are you in a condition of perfect equilibrium?" asked the master.

"I think so," said the disciple, who had prayed religiously and practiced good deeds.

"When someone insults you, do you still feel injured? When you receive praise, does your heart expand with pleasure?"

The would-be disciple thought for a moment and replied somewhat sheepishly: "Yes, I suppose I do feel hurt when insulted and proud when praised."

"Well then, go out and practice detachment from worldly pain and pleasure for a few more years. Then come back and I will teach you how to meditate."

That novice most surely did not pack up and move off to a cave to fast his ego into submission, for the codes and daily practices of traditional Judaism were all he needed to guide him toward egolessness. The prayer over his morning bread reminded him of the divine ground upon which his sustenance rested. He could lose his self-importance in observing the "miracle" of ordinary acts like breathing, eating, sleeping, making love to his wife, and trading with his neighbor. With a strongly concentrated mind, right in the middle of everyday life, the Jewish novice mystic prepared himself for enlightenment by climbing a spiritual ladder which, though rooted in the earth, would inevitably lead him to God. Undistracted observation of the commandments eventually humbled his ego to the point where he actually experienced a state called "Awe" in the continued presence of the Almighty. "Awe" would gradually turn to "Love," and "Love" to "Cleaving." *Love the Lord thy God . . . hearken to His voice, and . . . cleave unto Him; for that is thy life and the length of thy days,* says the author of Deuteronomy, a pronouncement that has been taken literally by Jewish mystics from biblical times onward. From this perspective, much of the Bible itself can be read as an instructive manual which charts the mystic way through withdrawal from sensory attachment (Ecclesiastes); confronts the heights and abysses of spiritual struggle (Psalms); and depicts the soul in union with its creator (Song of Songs).

The Maggid of Mezerich, a brilliant eighteenth-century Hasidic philosopher, puts it this way:

> A man should actually detach his ego from his body until he has passed through all the worlds and become one with God, till he disappears entirely out of the bodiless world.

His disciple, Shneur Zalman, called this process *bittul ha-yesh,* annihilation of the desiring self. Nevertheless, Jewish mystics are a paradoxical combination of spirituality and earthiness. Jews by nature are practical, grounded on the earth. They know almost instinctively that what goes up must come down and that, however "illusory," this world is a "university for the soul." Walking with your feet on the ground and your head in the sky is a tricky business. When the teacher demands that the disciple annihilate his ego out in the market place, he is planting him on the first and lowest branch of a tree whose roots consist of our world of human beings, animals, plants, minerals, pain, suffering, joy, procreation, and death—and whose highest branches culminate in the silent unknown and unknowable dwelling of the Infinite. Moreover, once he has learned to make his way comfortably on the root level of the tree, the Jewish mystic will eventually bear the responsibility for unifying the highest world with the lowest. He is expected to be engaged in social, political, family, and community life and at the same time to live in perfect undistracted communion with God.

For the Jew, community and religious observance are one. The mystic cannot isolate himself from his fellow men even in his esoteric practices, for the core of his faith, the divine revelation at Sinai, appeared not to one man, but to a community numbering six hundred thousand souls. The Jewish mystical experience has remained communal ever since. Suffering and persecution have infused it with hopes for messianic redemption; exile has imbued it with nationalism. When foreign tyrants were not busy exterminating the Jewish community, then false Messiahs and internal heresy seekers were doing their best to destroy the mystic vision from within. In the seventeenth century Smyrna-born Sabbatai Zevi, a self-proclaimed Messiah, succeeded in uprooting entire Jewish communities throughout Europe and the Near East. Envisioning immediate redemption at his hands, ecstatic bands followed their manic-depressive leader to Turkey. Those who returned home often found themselves broken, penniless nomads. Those who continued in their blind belief turned to license and apostasy. In the name of mystical redemption, Sabbatai Zevi (who finally himself converted to Islam) almost succeeded in destroying Jewish mysticism once and for all.

For more than a hundred years after this debacle, true followers of the mystical tradition practiced in secret, until, in the eighteenth century, they emerged as European Hasidim. And then, during the decaying Hasidic dynasties which followed, cults again sprang up around one master, a *tzaddik* whose supply of divine grace was believed powerful enough to transform an entire community of moonstruck devotees. Men threw up their jobs, donned exotic clothing, and exhibited exotic behavior in the name of their *tzaddik;* they carried him through the streets on a palanquin and let their families go in want, without even the basic necessities, in order to serve the needs of the master. This kind of worship was very un-Jewish, since Jews traditionally find it hard to submit to the absolute mental tyranny of another human being. Great teachers have always been revered among them, but the Jew was never to kneel before a "graven image"—even if it was the projected saintly image of his spiritual master. Yet the Jews continued to display a penchant for teacher worship that is still apparent today.

Because of its communal nature, Jewish mystical practice presents a double burden: one must not only learn to cleave to God, but he must take the entire community, the entire creation, with him! And, in order not to destroy them en route, he must be perfect. With Moses as his model, the Jewish mystic must concentrate on God in his every daily act, with his every breath; but he must always come down from the "high place" and live among the people as well. By "yoking" himself to God he develops a power of love so great that he brings the godly influx into this imperfect world of men.

From the earliest times the practice of Jewish mysticism has been secret. In eleventh-century Spain a philosopher named Ibn Gabirol labeled these secret oral teachings "Kabbalah," or *tradition.* All Jewish mystical practice since then falls under the heading of "Kabbalah." But that should not mislead us, for the same spiritual life style and practice, the same involvement with community predominated regardless of time or culture long before the eleventh century of the Common Era. But the Kabbalists did their work only too well. Fearful of persecution from within and without the Jewish community, they buried an already esoteric tradition even deeper. The complicated diagrams and mystic texts that pass for Kabbalah today were often deliberately distorted in order to confuse the uninitiated eye. The tradition was itself passed down orally from master to disciple, thus insuring its integrity on the one hand and providing personal guidance on the other. In the thirteenth century in Spain much of it came to light in written form in a book called *Zohar* (Book of Splendor), which supposedly described the exploits and teachings of Rabbi Simeon bar Yohai, a first-century sage and master Kabbalist. Yet even this "explication" of kabbalistic beliefs and practices leaves both laymen and scholars hardly more informed about its practical application than they were before.

Kabbalah is not an intellectual discipline, nor is it—like the Talmud—a rational exegesis of Jewish Law. It is first and foremost a mystical practice, but one that is fully dependent on, and integrated with, Judaism as a whole. Trying to practice kabbalistic "meditation" without understanding its foundation in the Torah (the Pentateuch) would be like trying to fly without wings. One cannot even begin to live the mystical life as a Jew without a knowledge of Hebrew, for the very stuff of its contemplation is the language of the Torah. Various Kabbalists have used the individual letters comprising chapter and verse as subjects for meditation. Contrary to most other spiritual disciplines which urge the seeker to get away from it all, to retire to a quiet place in the country and meditate, the Jewish mystic is urged to start living in the midst of worldly activity in a new way. He begins with the advice of the talmudic sages who urge him to "eat bread with salt, drink water moderately, sleep on the ground, lead a close life, and study hard."

Different masters have interpreted this injunction in different ways. The dispersion of the Jews has made a consistent school of mystical practice almost impossible. The wonder is that, despite the scattered and often culturally incompatible populations, Jewish mystical practices are so similar. Hebrew as a common language undoubtedly helped. Ancient mystics placed great emphasis on visionary experience and contemplation. Sephardic Jews concentrated more on the prophetic aspects of meditation and on the Jews as a holy community. European mystics elevated prayer to divine status. With the Pentateuch and Laws as its guide, the Kabbalah has flourished—sometimes darkly and sometimes brilliantly—for over five thousand years. Often so incorporated into the everyday life of the Jews that it has gone unnoticed, mysticism once again appears to be enjoying a popular resurgence. Since it is almost entirely centered on the words of its great masters and on their personal approaches to its implementation in Jewish life, the Kabbalah can best be understood through the teachings themselves.

"God travels incognito."

**An anonymous atheist
on tour in Israel**

I
The Mystic Life

1

The Preparatory Phase: Cultivating Awe

THE HIDDEN GARDEN

Study of Kabbalah is likened to entering a splendid but dangerous garden. Open the first gate and you find yourself confronted by massive vines and creepers, moving flowers, golden birds, and talking butterflies. Enter the next gate and you find the entire scene vanishes; now you are surrounded by a mirage of sunlit water which, upon closer inspection, actually turns out to be the marble foyer of a great palace. Open another gate and you enter the world of disembodied sound, where the soft beating of wings announces that you have reached the realm of *Ofanim,* angelic beings in the shape of wheels. Every gate of this garden leads deeper into hallucinatory visions, snares that entrap the unwary wanderer at each turning.

The successful pilgrim, having integrated his psychological, ethical, and spiritual selves, will continue until he reaches a clear space. Here grows a tree whose branches are made of ten differently colored spheres, each representing an ascending "world," or level of spiritual perception. Having come upon this "tree of life," the mystic knows that he has reached the point where he is truly ready to climb. The gates have led him into the hidden *Pardes,* the garden in which there grows the sacred tree which marks his ascent to God.

Jewish sages warn all but the perfectly stable, perfectly ethical man away from this place. The letters of the Hebrew word *Pardes*, they say, contain the clue to the secret contained there: P represents *Peshat*, the simple, exterior meaning of the Torah; R stands for *Remez*, the homiletical meaning; D is *Drush*, the allegorical meaning; and S is *Sod*, its secret, or innermost, meaning. To illustrate the nature of the perilous journey through the "garden" of Jewish mystical life, talmudic rabbis tell the story of four great sages, Ben Azai, Ben Zoma, Ben Abuyah, and Rabbi Akiva. These scholars actually lived and taught in Palestine during the first centuries of the Common Era. All were renowned legalists at the central Jewish academy of learning at Yavneh after the second destruction of the Temple in Jerusalem. According to historical accounts, Ben Zoma became insane, Ben Abuyah turned apostate traitor, Ben Azai died in his prime, and Akiva, at ninety, became an enlightened saint and martyr.

Legend relates that each of the four "entered *Pardes*," that is, embraced the mystical life. Rabbi Akiva, the oldest and best prepared, was first to achieve superconscious states. However, on his "return" to waking consciousness, he warned the other three not to succumb to the illusions their minds would create along the way.

"When you enter near the pure stones of marble, do not say, 'Water! Water!' for the Psalms tells us, 'He who speaks falsehood will not be established before My Eyes.'"

The saintly Rabbi Ben Azai "gazed and died," for his soul so longed for its source that it instantly shed the physical body upon entering the light.

Ben Abuyah, whose intellectual confusion had not been sufficiently cleared away, gazed and, seeing not one God but two, instantly became an apostate.

Ben Zoma looked and lost his mind, for he had not reconciled ordinary life with visionary experience.

Only Rabbi Akiva, the man of perfect equilibrium, entered and left in peace.

For the Kabbalist, thought, deed, and goal are directly related; therefore the more he refines his mind, body, and soul, the more he resembles God. Since he believes that man is literally created in the image of God, the mystic works to polish himself until he becomes so brilliantly clear that he reflects nothing but God. "Union with the Absolute" in this case is a matter of "like attracting like." The more godly a man becomes, the more divinity shines through him. On this first branch of the spiritual tree, the entire revealed world is the Kabbalist's polishing tool. He distills God's presence from the stars, people, food—from all of life around him. As his senses are further refined, he will become conversant with the ethereal world of angelic beings, pure color and sound, until finally he reaches the unmanifest level of awareness called *devekuth,* cleaving to God, the highest state attainable by human consciousness.

BAHYA BEN JOSEPH IBN PAQUDA: "KNOW GOD WITH YOUR HEART"

The Book of Direction to the Duties of the Heart, Bahya ben Joseph Ibn Paquda's eleventh-century manual for mystics, emphasizes the revealed aspect of God "in connection with the sky and the earth, the world and the winds." Bahya encourages his students to begin with a study of nature before moving on to more abstract subjects. Bliss ungrounded in physical reality is not bliss but delusion, insists the Jewish master: "Whenever you imagine Him in some form or think of Him as resembling something, you should endeavor to examine His meaning further . . . until the image is driven away from your mind and you reach Him by way of demonstration only." The Jew studies the image, extracts its divine content, and thus comes to see God everywhere.

A judge in the rabbinical court at Saragossa, Spain, during the first half of the eleventh century, Bahya concerned himself primarily with applying Jewish Law to mystical practice. Influenced by the ascetic philosophy and techniques of his contemporaries, the Moslem Sufi mystics, Bahya injected an esoteric cast to traditional Jewish ethics. He was critical of the rabbis who paid attention only to the outward law and ignored its spiritual content. Very little is known about his own life and practices; his reticence about revealing his system publicly is apparent in the introduction to *The Duties of the Heart*. But the spiritual void in Judaism was obviously so great at the time of his judgeship that it provoked him to write. Familiar with the great Arabic philosophers of his time, a Neoplatonic mystic who nevertheless remained impeccably Jewish, Bahya synthesized the contemplative asceticism of the East with common-sense Judaism. His own sincere piety and love of God shine through every word of his emotionally charged teaching: know God with your heart.

The mind, according to Bahya, should function as a discriminating corroborator of direct religious *experience* and not of blind belief or tradition.

He divides his practice of "self-reckoning" into ten gates corresponding to what he considers the ten levels in a man's spiritual life. (The "gate" as an image of graduated mystical experience is most favored by Jews.) First, and most important, is realizing the unity of God in the plurality of creation. To this end, Bahya recommends studying the active workings of the Divine in nature—from unicellular organisms to man. Removing himself from his own desires and aversions, the mystic contemplates nature as a scientist would. First he fixes his attention on the separate elements: fire, air, earth, and water; then he studies them in combinations like gas, ice, minerals, and plants. Next he contemplates man the organism. He might, for example, consider his own development, picturing himself as an embryo in his mother's womb and imagining the growth process from fetus to adulthood in his mind's eye, somewhat like a slow-motion film. From an almost microscopic journey into his every organ and limb, he proceeds to contemplate mental functions like memory, speech, and thought, and then the emotions emanating from those functions: shame, love, anger, and so on.

5

This intensive study of the organic world, says Bahya, will bring a man naturally to full understanding of the metaphysical, philosophical, social, artistic, and moral systems that prevail on earth. True comprehension of his own marvelous physical being—his body's transformation of food into energy and life, the subtle and miraculous workings of the breath—will enable the student to understand the ethereal body to which his animal, instinctual self is tied, the nexus where body and soul are joined through nerves, blood, and breath.

Bahya advises his disciples to conduct this minute investigation into every single aspect of nature: the relationship between seed, soil, and the growth of fully developed plants; the changing colors of light at dawn and dusk, the seasons, even the insect crawling across the wall in front of him may elevate a man to the level of Awe.

The second gate represents the proper worship of God resulting from these contemplations. His new understanding of creation now evokes in the disciple the wish to adhere to the Jewish Law in an entirely new spirit. No longer motivated by fear of punishment or desire for heavenly rewards, he serves God out of pure gratitude for His gifts. Performing the *mitzvah*, or divine precept, of eating only prescribed foods, for example, is a natural outgrowth of his study of animal life. Now, rather than following out of habit or obedience, he adopts the *mitzvah* quite naturally, in true humility and understanding of its purpose. The whole creation vibrates with godly energy. But he does not abandon himself to blissful renunciation of his affairs; firmly planted on the "middle path," he avoids asceticism as much as sensuality. At this point in the practice, Bahya's disciple is ready to enter the gate of Trust, the third gate. Here he will cultivate the equilibrium that is so important for further progress on the spiritual tree. He learns to confide in God alone and to trust the divine universal order so deeply that he feels he lacks nothing. The greatness and wonder of the universe have proven God's wisdom to him; now he can accept that wisdom as reflected in his own daily life. Passing through the fourth gate, Acceptance, he grows satisfied with his lot; even trials and sufferings help him, expanding his heart to allow more of God in. But he doesn't become fatalistic about life. God provides, but the disciple must work, earn money, and refrain from violating his body and its needs.

The fifth gate, Hypocrisy, offers him a chance to test his sincerity. Beyond its lies the realm of doubt, anger, and nihilism. Should he cling perfectly to his hard-won faith, Bahya assures him, he will pass through unharmed into the sixth gate, Humility. Now the mystic finds that he is less critical of others, that at last he can bear insults without feeling their sting. He and his achievements are no longer one. The fine house, beautiful wife, successful sons exist outside of him on their own.

At the seventh gate he encounters his past sins. Repentance enables him to confront his actions honestly and to empty his heart in prayer. Determined to change his destructive behavior in the future, he confides openly in God, and pleads for aid in eliminating his sins. Open pleading, supplication, sighing, and tears are very much part of Jewish mystical prayer. Medieval Hasidim in Germany used to stand for an hour in silent preparation before uttering even the first line of the liturgy. Taking this very personal realtionship with God a step further, Rebbe Levi Isaac of Berdichev, an eighteenth-century Hasid, stood at the altar of the synagogue on the High Holy Days and pleaded aloud with God to spare His people suffering, as a lawyer would plead a case before a judge. Other mystics, less inclined to public display, sat in private meditation chambers in their homes or out in the fields, weeping and calling to God.

Bahya, like all Jewish mystics, believed that by enacting interior states, concretizing them, so to speak, one was unifying the spiritual with the physical. This is a very important concept in Judaism: there cannot be any progress on the spiritual path without concommitant physical behavior. Therefore, if one repents internally, says Bahya, he must enact that repentance in his external life. He cannot procrastinate, saying, "I'll eliminate that trait later." Deathbed repentance enjoys a very low rank in Judaism. Acknowledgment of one's "sins" must be followed by repentance in word, thought, and deed. Bahya illustrates the importance of this gate in the following story.

Hoping to create a path across a stream, a traveler threw all his silver coins into the water. As he approached the stream, however, he found that all his coins but one had sunk to the bottom. He managed to rescue that one coin and used it to pay the ferryman, who rowed him across. Repentance, says Bahya, is like that last coin. When all of life's treasures are gone, it alone will help a man across the waters of life.[1]

Passing through the eighth gate, Examination of the Soul, the mystic attempts to purify himself to the point where he will "see without eyes, hear without ears, speak without tongue, perceive without the sense of perception, and deduce without reason . . ." The inner gate of this path is reserved for those who are willing to seclude themselves from the world in meditation. Although this appears to conflict with the anti-ascetic bias of Jewish Law, it is nevertheless a stage of mystical practice which cannot be avoided by that small group of superior human beings whose desire to see God exceeds even their love for His creation. Prophets and saints abound in Judaism, and it is to these that Bahya now addresses himself. Like the ancient biblical prophets, certain human beings will be compelled to turn away from the world. Making their homes in deserts and forests as hermits, they will seek the vision of God alone. Others, of a more sociable temperament, will seclude themselves in special secret rooms at home, dwelling on God in ecstatic prayer. More traditional Jews will seek to remain in the world, participating in its ac-

---

[1] Since Bahya attributes this story to "the ancients," one wonders if he hasn't perhaps adapted for his own purposes a Hindu tale designed to illustrate the folly of acquiring miraculous powers. A disciple once came bragging to his teacher that he had spent twelve years on the shores of a stream perfecting his psychic abilities until one morning he found that he could walk across the water without even getting his feet wet. The teacher looked at him sadly and said: "What a pity that you wasted so much time when one silver coin could have paid the ferryman to row you across."

tivities according to the precepts and Law, but they will exclude all luxury from their lives. Living according to the injunction of the talmudic sages, they will eat and sleep sparingly and will devote themselves to studying the Torah.

Abstinence, the ninth gate, becomes more or less necessary in proportion to the nature of the community in which a man finds himself. If the Jews are surrounded by hedonistic nations, then the ascetic mode of life is essential to their moral survival. Since the entire system outlined in *The Duties of the Heart* is designed to distance a man from his ego and to prepare him for his eventual meeting with God, its implementation can only succeed in proportion to his self-discipline. If the world around him is utterly corrupt, he might perhaps find it easier to retire to a quiet community of like-minded people. If he has entered the tenth gate of Saintliness, he may remain in the midst of the hubbub and provide a mainstay for other seekers.

If he adheres to the lessons of the various gates and makes them part of himself, the mystic ultimately leaves the realm of Awe for the more deeply personal realm of Love. Here his soul so longs for its source that he is capable of the greatest earthly sacrifices, even of life itself. Like the saint found sleeping in the desert, who, when wakened and asked by a traveler if he didn't fear the lions all about, having passed through the final gate, Bahya's disciple will also be able to answer: "I should feel ashamed of my God did I entertain fear of any being besides Him."

Desert solitude, however, provides a ready backdrop for visionary experience. Bahya's ascetic teaching was actually implemented as a practicable communal system five centuries later by the mystic brotherhood occupying the northern Galilee town of Safed.

SAFED: THE JEWISH SHANGRI-LA

Safed still perches on the face of a green mountain overlooking the Hula Valley. Ascending the winding road to the city on a misty morning, the traveler sees nothing at first but low-hanging cloud and mossy-green downs that might vaguely remind him of the Scottish highlands. The air, thin and crisp, assures him that he has indeed left behind the balmy, palm-lined shores of the Sea of Galilee for a new country. Suddenly the clouds are dispelled by a bright shaft of sunlight, revealing a clump of ocher-colored houses that jut forth precariously from the mountain itself. Safed is a natural mystic's retreat, the perfect landscape for cultivating Awe, an ethereal town that could just as well have been a tiny Tibetan enclave or the setting for an isolated monastery in the Himalayan foothills; a Jewish Shangri-La. And so it was, once.

Today its narrow winding streets and dusty roads house an artists' colony; four centuries ago Kabbalists performed miracles on those streets and, dressed in white, danced, with vine leaves in their hair, toward their blue-painted synagogues on the Sabbath day. The cats are still there, innumerable dozens of them, seated, licking their paws, in the tiny arched doorways of the Kabbalists' houses and reputed by local residents to be *gilgulim* (incarnations) of kabbalistic familiars who still watch over the town. The synagogues are still there, too— empty, save for their oriental carpets, circular benches, and graceful pewter chandeliers. The mahogany altars, placed, according to Sephardic tradition, at the center of the room, are beautifully burnished, kept in perfect condition by the ancient beadles who cherish every vestige of the town's past. The graveyard, with its stellar grouping of headstones commemorating kabbalistic masters buried there, lies on a craggy slope in full view of the houses, almost as if to remind their current occupants of the illustrious Cordoveros, Lurias, and Caros who lived there once.

Emulating the mystics of old, the contemporary Hasid will prostrate himself on the grave of the one they called the "*Ari,*" greatest Kabbalist of them all. Closing his eyes, he will remain bowed in silent meditation, hoping to unite a spark of his own soul with the deathless spirit of the master. Yet, although a certain aura of sanctity and peace cling there still, he knows as he departs that the heyday of Jewish communal mysticism, the glory of Safed, has indeed passed—perhaps forever.

Though a sizable Jewish community existed there from ancient times, thanks to the Spanish expulsion of Jews the population of Safed swelled in the fifteenth and sixteenth centuries into a thriving economic, intellectual, and spiritual center. In 1607 Shlomel of Moravia, author of a biography of Isaac Luria, the Ari, could write:

> Here live great scholars, saints, and men of action . . . None among them is ashamed to go to the well and draw water and carry the pitcher on his shoulders, or go to the market to buy bread, oil, and vegetables. All the work in the house is done by themselves.[2]

Modeled on the Essene commune system, life in Safed represented the perfect socialist ideal of co-operation. It was a place where Isaac Luria, the greatest of the town's masters, contributed huge sums to its treasury from his family's trade in textiles, and where Spanish-born Joseph Caro, whose name is synonymous with the entire halakhic (legal) tradition of Judaism, could function as an inspired mystic by night and practical attorney by day. Caro, in fact, was "ordered" there by a divine decree which he had received while in ecstatic trance. In 1536 he arrived in Palestine from Constantinople and immediately settled into the thriving community of artisans, farmers, tradesmen, and teachers that welcomed him in Safed. His own yeshivah was attended by such illustrious scholars as Moses Cordovero (1522–70), brother-in-law and disciple of the famous Solomon Alkabez, an outstanding mystical writer and, at that time, the leading Kabbalist of Safed.

Under Alkabez' leadership, a group calling itself the *Chaverim* (Comrades) met regularly at the graves of dead saints, where they conducted scriptural discourses and group meditation. It was Caro the lawyer who drew up the articles of their

[2] Quoted in Solomon Schechter, "Safed in the Sixteenth Century," *Studies in Judaism*, p. 232.

association. During these meetings, Alkabez enjoined the members to maintain constant and undistracted attentiveness to the Torah, both in thought and in enactment of its precepts. To turn their hearts into "the abode of the *Shekhinah*" (immanent presence and female aspect of God) they were taught how to continually purify their minds and bodies by refraining from anger, gossip, cruelty to animals, swearing, and hypocrisy. The *Chaverim* agreed not to indulge in feasting except on the Sabbath and other high religious occasions; each man vowed to share in the sufferings of his neighbor as well as in his joys.

Forming the basis for all kabbalistic communities to come, the Safed mystics outlined a schedule which included meeting for one or two hours a day for spiritual discussion, and on Fridays, for a general review of the deeds they had accomplished during the week. After these spiritual conclaves, the *Chaverim* gathered their families and went out into the streets en masse, extending joyous welcome to the "Sabbath Queen." At home they were careful to indoctrinate their children with the same spiritual fervor, reciting grace at table very clearly, allowing every member of the family to repeat and savor the meaning of each word. Before retiring, they performed an ancient mental exercise, outlined by Philo, a first century C.E. Hellenic Jewish philosopher, which entailed examining the activities and conversations of the day backward—a device for detached self-reckoning that immediately revealed each transgression and omission of the divine and earthly precepts in the Torah. Though they came from many different parts of Europe and the Near East and therefore spoke different languages, the students were encouraged by Alkabez to converse in Hebrew among themselves, particularly on the Sabbath. Each *Chaver* had the right to rebuke his fellow when he found him in error, but the admonished party was not to reply.

Other Safed societies included penitents and ascetics of every variety. When Joseph Caro arrived in 1536, he found an entire town devoted primarily to spiritual life and only incidentally to earning a living. Some citizens fasted, others prayed all night, still others practiced strict vegetarianism. Yet the asceticism prevailing in Safed never emphasized mortification for its own sake; putting the Torah into practice was its primary aim. Thus, citizens distributed charity daily; orphans were immediately adopted and raised by more fortunate families; holidays were entirely communal, entirely mystical occasions for rejoicing.

Working on the psyche lay beyond exercising ethical behavior on the practical level of daily interaction. To nourish the spiritual center in the heart and to cultivate the first level of mystic consciousness—Awe—the *Chaverim* of Safed followed a course of instruction laid out by the brilliant scholar and teacher Moses Cordovero. Imitating the thirteen divine attributes recited in his daily prayers, the mystic attempted to reinforce in himself the following pattern of egoless behavior:

1. Forbearance in the face of insult.
2. Patience in enduring evil.
3. Pardon, to the point of erasing the evil suffered.
4. Total identification with his neighbor.
5. Complete absence of anger, combined with appropriate action.
6. Mercy, to the point of recalling only the good qualities of his tormentor.
7. Eliminating all traces of vengefulness.
8. Forgetting suffering inflicted on himself by others and remembering the good.
9. Compassion for the suffering without judging them.
10. Truthfulness.
11. Mercy beyond the letter of the Law with the good.
12. Assisting the wicked to improve without judging them.
13. Remembering all human beings always in the innocence of their infancy.

MOSES CORDOVERO'S "THIRTEEN DIVINE ATTRIBUTES"

Cordovero taught that it was not only within the power of the mystic to absorb or forfeit these thirteen divine attributes himself, but that each time he neglected any one of them, he would be withdrawing them from the entire world as well! Because concrete images were more easily reinforced than abstract terms like "humility" and "compassion," Cordovero taught each of the *Chaverim* to picture his own body as an analogue of the great cosmic tree of life which condensed them all. When the disciple wished to focus his attention on humility, for example, he could think first of the highest sphere on the tree, the *Crown* of God, and then associate it with his own head. In this way, he would always remember not to walk with his head held arrogantly in the air, away from the gaze of other human beings. Secondly, he would automatically come to associate the head with the brain, or seat of thought inside, and thus always collect his thoughts and direct them to God. Picturing the forehead made him associate to the idea of maintaining an open and pleasant demeanor. The ears reminded him to stay alert to useful information, and to shut out slander and other useless chatter. Eyes stood for mercy when he pictured them open, and strength against temptation when he pictured them closed. Kindness traveled with every breath inhaled through the nose, while anger was represented by snorting. A radiant face symbolized cheerfulness, sweetness, and the absence of harsh judgment. The mouth represented wisdom dispensed without slander or cruelty.

By embodying these divine qualities beyond their usual human limits, the mystic sought to become a pure vessel, ready for still higher practices and knowledge. Cordovero urged his students to work slowly, making humility "the key to all." If his prayers aimed at nothing less than the *Crown* of the tree, the symbol of perfect humility, then the mystic was expected to behave humbly at every moment when he was not at prayer. The *Crown*, being associated with Nothingness (God without form), is the essence of humility as we know it in our world. To the Kabbalist, who actually linked his every waking thought and deed to this highest and subtlest form of it, humility therefore became a perfect instrument for the ego annihilation that preceded structured meditation.

Cordovero assured the *Chaverim* that daily practice of the "thirteen divine attributes" would perpetuate an easy, natural ascent on the cosmic tree. It would, he said, be quite effortless for a man without an ego to react mercifully in the face of pain inflicted upon him by his neighbor, for there was, in fact, no *thing* of himself left to be hurt! Of course the *Chaver* had to be wary of the inevitable worldly distractions that would deflect him from his goal, the lure of honor being the worst by far. So he could contemplate, and thereby *honor*, God's creation as an emblem of his own temptation in reverse.

THE TREE OF LIFE

The cosmic tree of life conveniently epitomized the emanation of God's "qualities" into the visible world of men:

THE COSMIC TREE

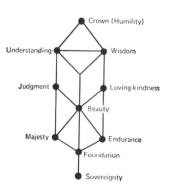

15

And since imitating God eventually led a man to direct knowledge of God, the Kabbalist exerted himself to perfect each quality on the tree. He was thus engaged in a continual contemplative flow between *Crown* and *Wisdom* in his mind and between humility and communication of spiritual wisdom in his actions. The function of *Understanding* was to provide him with a weapon against worldliness. Again, thinking of the tree as his own body, Cordovero's student divided the left and right "branches" into "feminine" (negative energy) and "masculine" (positive energy) aspects of himself and, by extension, the universe. Where the *Crown* had been neuter, above all created things, the descending spheres now assumed color, gender, form, and sound. Fixing his attention on the sphere of *Loving-kindness*, with its appropriate color, angelic guardian, and prayer, the *Chaver* appropriated a model for projecting mercy into every possible life situation. The transition between the contemplative mental image and its physical effect no doubt took the space of an instant. Eventually, they became so integrated that the Kabbalist no longer differentiated at all between contemplation and ordinary daily activity. He had, as it were, *become* the qualities *Crown, Wisdom, Understanding,* and so on.

Until he was ready for total ascetic isolation, it was the mystic's job to co-ordinate the opposing energies on the "tree" of his own body. All sexual and aggressive impulses, for example, stemmed from the sphere of *Judgment* on the left. Far from ignoring or suppressing sex or aggression, however, the *Chaver* learned to unify his "male" and "female" selves in marriage and in work. Once he had successfully integrated these impulses with his spiritual pursuit, said Cordovero, the Kabbalist could "turn them all toward the service of God to bind them to the Right." This "binding" exercise (known as *yichud*), which only came after much rigorous practice, meant that a man had reached the stage where he could take not only himself to God, but all the worlds with him.

Cordovero also taught his students how to recognize the

cosmic cycles beyond their own bodies and minds. Each of God's qualities ruled a different time of day; thus, for example, the mystic went to sleep with his mind focused on *Sovereignty,* the ruler of night. At midnight, he rose, washed, and contemplated the spiritual substance of the Torah in the form of the bride of God, *Shekhinah.* At dawn, before entering the synagogue, he fastened his attention on the three patriarchs—Abraham (embodied in *Loving-kindness*), Isaac (embodied in *Judgment*), and Jacob (embodied in *Beauty*). More advanced students were able to co-ordinate these images with their corresponding body parts and with synagogue liturgy simultaneously. The ability to combine such complicated mental exercises with physical activity provided the teacher an ample yardstick for measuring the degree and intensity of each student's power of concentration, or *kavanna.* By the time he had completed the course, the Kabbalist had so effaced his individuality that his personal life cycle had become indistinguishable from that of the impersonal universe. Using the ritual obligations imposed upon him by the Torah within the framework of his workaday word, the *Chaver* of Safed attempted to transform his life into one prolonged gaze at the Infinite.

"This," says Cordovero, "is [the Kabbalist's] daily cycle in accord with the cycle of the spheres, so that he is attached, ever, to the dominating light . . . And this is a comprehensive method by which man can bind himself always to holiness so that the *Crown* of the *Shekhinah* nevermore departs from his head."

ISAAC LURIA: THE "LION" OF SAFED

Cordovero, Alkabez, and the others merely set the stage for the arrival in 1570 of the sublime teacher of teachers, Isaac Luria, the "Ari," the Lion, of Safed. At this time, Chayim Vital (1543–1620), a scholarly rabbi living in Damascus, was suddenly beset by visions announcing the appearance of an avatar in Safed. Following his intuition, Vital journeyed there and found that his visions had proven correct. Almost as soon as he had arrived, the Ari (a permutation of the name "Rabbi Isaac Ashkenazi") was acclaimed the undisputed leader of the mystic school of Safed. Though his tenure lasted only six years, he completely revised the practice of Jewish mysticism from that point on.

Born in Jerusalem in 1534, Isaac Luria (a descendant of a German family and therefore called "Ashkenazi", to denote his Western ancestry) was no ordinary child. Before the Ari's birth, his father was visited by the prophet Elijah, who announced: "Through him shall be revealed the teaching of the Kabbalah to the world." At the circumcision, the child's father saw the prophet himself standing among the congregants in the crowded synagogue.

When he was only eight years old, the boy already proved himself to be a talmudic genius. His father died not long after the Ari's eighth year, and the family moved to the home of a wealthy uncle in Cairo. His mother's brother, recognizing the boy as a prodigy, adopted him and enrolled him with a tutor named Bezalel Ashkenazi (his true master, and, according to the Ari himself, the real source of his own name), who taught him until he was fifteen, at which point the boy married his cousin (and stepsister) and terminated his studies. At seventeen the Ari was initiated into the Kabbalah.

One day a traveler, who had arrived in Cairo on business, joined the usual throng of worshipers at Luria's synagogue for the afternoon service. The young scholar's curiosity was aroused when he saw the man reading his prayers from a manuscript depicting kabbalistic interpretations of the liturgy. Luria approached the man and questioned him about the manuscript. Embarrassed by the inquiry, the businessman protested that he was only an ignorant Marrano, a baptized Spanish Jew secretly adhering to Judaism, who could not even read the letters of the volume he was holding. Luria pleaded with him to sell the manuscript, since it could be of no real value to a man who couldn't read it. At first the man refused, but he eventually agreed to sell the volume with the provision that Luria prevail on his behalf with his influential father-in-law on a tax matter.

The book was none other than the *Zohar* (Book of Splendor), which Luria studied laboriously for the next eight years. When he was not as successful in comprehending its contents as he had originally hoped, Luria set himself on an ascetic course prescribed for him by what he called a "heavenly impetus." Retreating in solitude to a small cottage on the banks of the Nile, he spent five days alone in constant study and meditation, returning to his family in the city for the Sabbath. Prayer, fasting, and the *Zohar* remained his only companions for two years, at the end of which, the prophet Elijah appeared in a vision to initiate him personally. Each night after that, the Ari found himself in the company of angelic hosts and great departed sages like Rabbi Simeon bar Yohai (purported author of the *Zohar*), Rabbi Akiva, and Rabbi Eleazar the Great. In addition, he could now read faces, deeds, the future, and the thoughts of others even before they had appeared. All the secrets of reincarnation were revealed to him during these nightly meetings. Thus, the Ari learned to differentiate between old souls and new ones; he read instantly their spiritual evolution or degeneration. In the flame of a candle he saw the future, located the souls of the righteous dead, even conversed and studied with them. Most impressive were his nightly communications with Elijah, from whom he derived—"mouth to ear"—his entire corpus of kabbalistic wisdom.

Eight visionary years passed; then, under the order of his celestial master, the Ari moved his family from Egypt to Safed. Elijah also announced to him that he was not to live very much longer, but that his final mission awaited him in the northern Galilee region.

Cordovero and the others welcomed him immediately. The two men struck up a mutual colleague-disciple relationship that soon gave way to the Ari's undisputed mastership. Though his son eventually became engaged to Joseph Caro's daughter, however, the new Lion of Safed and the ecstatic legalist maintained respectful but cool relations. Chayim Vital, whose prophecy had been corroborated by the master's arrival, became his closest disciple, as well as his biographer, scribe, and publicist. The Ari himself proved so ethereal that he needed a more earthly vehicle, like the active Vital, to transmit his message in writing.

"It is impossible, because all things are interrelated," the Ari said once. "I can hardly open my mouth to speak without feeling as though the sea had burst its dams and overflowed. How then shall I express what my soul has received, and how can I put it down in a book?" That remained the task of Chayim Vital, who, laboring under a stricture against note taking, nevertheless managed to collate the entire Lurianic system of mystical bits and pieces into a brilliantly unified whole.

Moses Cordovero died in his forty-eighth year, leaving the kabbalistic community bereft of its most lucid explicator. At his funeral bier, the Ari saw a pillar of fire accompanying the great soul that, according to him, had been an incarnation of Abraham's servant Eleazar. With Cordovero gone, the *Chaverim* changed their name to the "Lion Cubs" in honor of the Ari. Soon organized within an enclosure consisting of a block of buildings housing dormitories and kitchens for the Cubs and their families, the group of twelve devoted themselves entirely to the new teaching. It was here that the Ari inaugurated his ideas about the universal mixture of good and evil interfering between man and God.

According to Luria, the task of the Kabbalist in his private meditations now encompassed the universe. Once the purified, humbled mind had attached itself to its divine source, it was obliged to plunge downward into the descending worlds with renewed strength and withdraw the holy sparks from the husks of matter encasing every being, flower, mineral, and demon inhabiting them. For this purpose, the Ari developed an entirely new system of concentration, depicting his elaborate mental exercises in the form of *kavannot* (contemplative symbols denoting specific visualizations) over the letters and phrases of the daily prayers.

Since performance of these exercises required the utmost purity of mind and body, the Ari initiated a parallel course of *tikkun* (correction). Certain prescribed formulas, given individually by the teacher to the disciple, were designed to cleanse his soul of its defects and thus prepare the way for purification of all that it reflected.

The dormitory experiment proved unsuccessful when the Cubs' families started squabbling over petty daily events. The Ari was severely disheartened when the news reached him, but the group, though no longer sharing living quarters, continued to function nonetheless. Members fell into one of two categories, each geared to match the extent of a man's knowledge and spiritual development. On his part, the Ari sought to further the idea that they were indeed all *members* of a large body which represented, organically, all their spiritual hopes and aspirations. Instructing them to keep this image in mind, he taught the Cubs to pray continuously for the good of their neighbors, advocating that they love them even more than they loved or cared for themselves, and, still further, that they love the whole of Israel even more. In their prayers, they were to dedicate themselves "for Israel, in Israel, and with Israel . . ." Thus, although the Ari advised his disciples to love all creatures without preference, he inadvertently initiated the nationalistic stance that characterized a great part of kabbalistic belief and practice for the next two hundred years. Some even go so far as to say that his "nationalism" opened the door to Sabbatai Zevi's destructive pseudo-messianic movement.

Yet the Ari himself did love all of creation without exception. He carefully avoided harming even insects and worms, insisting that these too would evolve through the course of transmigrating souls. Even inanimate things, as he saw them, could be communicated with through the language of the spirit. For this reason every word in Lurianic prayer is invested with mysteries that transcend all attempts at literal interpretation. He elevated the written concentration exercises to an exalted degree, inscribing them in Sephardic prayer books that, two centuries after his death, also served as meditation manuals for the Baal Shem Tov's ecstasy-seeking European Hasidim. In the Ari's system, real prayer could only be uttered by a pure man who had disappeared into the infinite reaches of the cosmic *Crown* even before he opened his mouth to utter God's praises. To this extent, the Ari's emphasis on simplicity, humility, and charity was even greater than Bahya's or Cordovero's. Exhibiting all these traits himself, the Ari inspired the Safed community, which never ceased to adore him for his unlimited generosity and personal sweetness.

Then, in 1572, he fell ill suddenly and died within three days. Joseph Caro died three years later. Chayim Vital returned to Damascus, where he died in 1620. Thus diminished, the great mystic community of Safed saw the end of its golden age.

Vital's records, kept secret until his death, were revealed and circulated against his known wishes. Thus, the Ari's teachings, as Gershom Scholem puts it, "became the common property of later Kabbalism."

Through Vital, we may glimpse into the purification instructions for a disciple about to perform the vast and complicated *yichud* (binding) meditation. Before entering the synagogue the disciple made an anonymous donation to a charitable cause. Then he bound his phylacteries to his head and arms and wore them throughout the entire morning prayer. Having mentally re-counted activities and thoughts of the day before, the Cub would ascertain whether or not he had scrupulously avoided harming any living thing. If the Ari had designated him a descendant of the soul of Cain, he was to avoid placing a knife on the table where he ate. Nor could he kill so much as a tick or a louse on his body or clothing. According to Vital's notes, the Ari taught his disciples how to walk, how to eat, and how to pray.

Following the Ari's instructions closely, the Cubs always placed salt on the table, but refrained from drinking water after eating. They kept their feet together while reciting blessings and worked hard to rid themselves of the habit of plucking hair from their beards when distracted. The Ari even gave them appropriate meditative chants for putting on Sabbath clothes! To inculcate "mindfulness," there were formulas for other nervous habits like finger fiddling and formulas designed to keep the disciple from carelessly dropping the thongs of his phylacteries on the floor during prayer. Each man was given a personal day of the week as a particularly salutary time for his spiritual progress, and a day out of each month when he was safe from harm and death. More than mere "lucky days," these periods were set aside for special "repentance" meditations designed to free a man's soul in preparation for his dying day. The Cub performed daily mental corrections, some as simple as repeating a phrase from Exodus 15: "I am God who heals you," in combination with a holy Name derived from the letters of the Tetragrammaton (YHVH).

The all-encompassing nature of his instructions reveals that the Ari wished to cure his disciples of the disease of worldliness with quick and sometimes even drastic methods. Perhaps it was because he knew he had only six years in which to teach them everything. Vital describes him as a "physician to the souls of his disciples," one who provided every one of them with the precisely appropriate correction for the deeds not only of his immediate life, but of past lives as well: "In that way . . . he recognized in each disciple which aspect of the soul was blemished and in which way to cleanse himself in order that he might receive the light."

The Ari was such a great spiritual master that he knew exactly where, and how high, on the cosmic tree each soul was located. In this vein, he explicated verses from the Torah to each of his students exactly at the moment when the student was intuitively ready to receive the meaning behind the verse and so further his spiritual ascent. The Cub would then speak the verse aloud, meditating on the Ari's explication as he did so.

The master presented his pupils with formulas for averting the "outside forces" that distracted their minds, formulas to remind them of their creation in God's own image, formulas to induce sounds and scents. When teaching how to meditate on the body, he told his Cubs to focus on the top of their heads only mentally, without chanting the holy names, for the *Crown* ruled in absolute silence. Walking outdoors, they were advised to imagine their legs as the spheres of *Endurance* and *Majesty* and their eyes as *Wisdom* and *Understanding*, always remembering that the body was a throne for the Holy Spirit. Some disciples even claimed to "fly" through the air by drawing down the light of a secret attribute called *Daath* (*Knowledge*), located between *Wisdom* and *Understanding* on the cosmic tree. There were numerous formulas for use in religious observances, holiday worship, and the execution of Jewish Law. Indeed, there were as many formulas for contemplative purposes as there were life experiences. "Everything," said the Ari, "depends on the intensity of your concentration and your attachment on high. Do not remove this from before your eyes." Motivated as they were by the intensity of the master's own spiritual example and dedicated to meditation on his *yichudim* (bindings), it is no surprise that the mystics of Safed compared themselves to "the angels in the heavens."

MOSES LUZZATTO AND HIS CIRCLE

Moses Chayim Luzzatto, a brilliant young eighteenth-century Kabbalist, regarded himself as a spiritual son of the Ari. For him, too, the interdependence of worlds, or planes of existence, also provided a convenient device for annihilating the ego and thereby expanding consciousness. How and when to influence the celestial messengers who mediated between God and His emanated worlds became a moral issue for the young Italian scholar.

Born in Padua in 1707, Luzzatto followed the typical course of a young Jew of privileged class, studying secular literature with the renowned Isaac Chayim Cohen Cantarini and religious works with the highly regarded Rabbi Isaiah Bassan. At an early age, however, Luzzatto developed an interest in Kabbalah and convinced his reluctant religious tutor to reveal some of its secrets to him. Growing dissatisfied with the unrelated shreds of mysticism that were formally available to him, Luzzatto embarked on a self-charted study of the forbidden works. Before long, he had gathered around himself a circle of like-minded university students, who convinced him to practice the Lurianic meditations inscribed in the mystical texts they were reading together in secret. Emulating the Safed mystics, the youthful master and his initial group of seven similarly privileged Jewish university students, drew up a code which they called "Regulations of the Circle," wherein they pledged themselves to:

> study the *Zohar* continuously without interruption, each member to read a portion in turn, from early morn until the hour for evening service, except on Sabbaths and holidays. The study of the *Zohar* is not for the purpose of the private [spiritual] advancement of any one of the members, not even for the purification of their sins, but is expressly and exclusively for the sake of "perfecting" the Holy *Shekhinah* and all Israel.

These lofty ideals were accompanied by intensive meditation on the Ari's *yichudim* (bindings) both day and night. Luzzatto later admitted to "burying" himself in the formulas, reciting them to himself mentally every fifteen minutes. Yet the rules of the Circle were fairly flexible despite their rigid-sounding code. Though the *Zohar* was read aloud continually by members throughout the day, non-members were permitted to relieve them at night. As a result, nine more young men joined, as they claimed, "in order to elevate the nation of Israel." Consciously imitating the Safed Kabbalists, they vowed communal concern for one another, a loving spirit, and a total commitment to the highest Truth. Mortifications of a sort were enacted in the form of collective fasts. In this spirit, they eventually instituted a round-the-clock reading of the *Zohar,* with each member taking turns at staying up. Some of the men read the Bible and Commentaries in addition; all willingly agreed to refrain from talking, greeting each other, or parting without the mention of God. Attempting to follow a monastic way of life without leaving the comfort of their parents' homes, the Circle members meditated in silence for long hours, walked with bowed heads, and observed the rabbinical laws to the letter.

"The whole subject of Kabbalah," said Luzzatto, "is to explain the nature of God, blessed be He, that He is absolutely and truly One, that He is unchangeable and that He has no bodily attributes . . ." The young philosopher-mystic expounded the superiority of experiential knowledge over mere intellectual speculation in spiritual matters:

> It is our duty to understand [Kabbalah] intelligently, not merely as a matter of belief, but so as to have our judgment's consent . . . When [the Torah] enters the soul, light comes with it like a sun's rays entering a house. Even more it is truly firelike . . . because all its words and letters are like coals seemingly extinguished, but when anyone begins to work on it, a great many-colored flame arises from every one of its letters. That is the knowledge hidden in each letter.

How to comprehend and apply the path of the Torah through self-knowledge became the basis of a preparatory system for mystics which Luzzatto called *The Path of the Just.* When a man had successfully trained and tested himself according to its stringent ethical and moral conditions, he was ready for the still higher "Way of God."

For this alone is the true good, and anything b
which people deem good is nothing but empt
worthlessness . . . [One] should persevere so as to u
self with the Blessed One by means of actions which
this end.

Luzzatto's stages leading to perfect union are taken from
the talmudic discourse of Rabbi Pinchas ben Yair, which emphasized:

Watchfulness
Zeal
Cleanliness
Separation
Purity
Saintliness
Humility
Fear of Sin, and
Holiness.

Talmudists referred to these traits as "a fence around the
Torah"; Luzzatto extended the idea further by taking his students beyond the border of human ethics into the divine
realm itself. To erase the worldly blindness imposed on him
by ego, Luzzatto's disciple (like his forerunner in Safed) was
bidden to set aside specific times of day and night for examination of his behavior, conducted with "the greatest regular-
ity." Reminiscent of Bahya's "self-reckoning" process, Luzzatto's introspection was augmented by corresponding study
of Scripture that was designed to elevate Watchfulness into a
contemplative state of Awe. Scripture combined with self-ex-
amination, he believed, would sharpen the Kabbalist's insight
into his own actions to such a point that Watchfulness would
soon become instinctive. For this reason he made sharp and
often critical distinctions between those zealous scholars who
"lost" themselves in the Torah and those who merely studied
it with heavenly rewards in mind. "Outer movements [like
egoless Torah study and introspection] awaken inner ones."

Though he began his career as a well-connected, married scholar, Luzzatto later lived, and preached, the mystic doctrine of rootlessness in the world and "rootedness in divine service." As the Kabbalist's craving for worldly honor decreased, so would his yearning for the Absolute increase, gradually drawing him toward more spiritual habits, practices, and people. This yearning marked his entry into the second stage, the practice of perfect Cleanliness, revealed through the mystic's now perfect sense of his own mental clarity and judgment. Pride, anger, and envy, in this stage, dropped from him as dead skin drops from a molting snake. So, too, the desire for wealth or fame. "For," Luzzatto assured him, "when [your] mind is alive with these things, it will survey all within its domain and bring forth new understanding from the wellspring of truth."

The stage of Separation marked the point where the disciple moved from mere ethical behavior toward Saintliness; the first operated within the ordered world of Jewish Law, the second took the mystic to a state of consciousness which was free of action altogether: "Upon the select few who desire to achieve closeness to the Blessed One, and to benefit thereby all those who depend on them, devolves the fulfillment of the saints' higher duties."

The Jewish saint, or *tzaddik*, lives completely detached from the pleasures of the world. Like the Buddhist bodhisattva, he is an enlightened being who has assumed human form and lives among other human beings in order to elevate them to divine status. Jewish mystics of the highest type were always *tzaddikim;* Saintliness remained the highest goal for those still on the path. To eliminate "worldliness," then, Luzzatto, like Bahya, advised his students to contemplate the deceptive nature of transitory "good." As he analyzed the qualities of each individual source of pleasure, the disciple came to see its reverse side, the impermanent lure. Such dehabituation practices eventually led him to "despise and decline [pleasure] as a severe and prolonged evil." Once revealed, this *truth* about the pointlessness of seeking pleasure and avoiding pain, pulled the disciple further away from materialism toward the simple life of contentment outlined in the Talmud. For those who could tolerate it, Luzzatto recommended total solitude; for the removal of worldly goods from before his eyes also removed the desire of them "from his heart."

Like all other Jewish mystics, Luzzatto, too, advocated moving along slowly, according to the ascending *madregot* (levels), appropriate to one's capacity. "Acquire a little today and [add] a little more tomorrow, until [you are] so habituated to it that it is second nature with [you]."

Purity meant scrutinizing every motive, even including those behind one's apparent good deeds. Enacting the *mitzvoth* (divine precepts) was meaningless if the Kabbalist bore even the hidden desire for spiritual reward. Purity meant desirelessness, disinterestedness, and perfectly selfless action. Ritual service directed toward a single goal, when performed with perfect concentration, helped to burn up any trace of the ego:

> The more time one devotes to thinking deeply into the matter in order to recognize the lowly nature of earthiness and its pleasures, the easier he will find it to purify his thoughts and his heart so that they have no recourse to the evil inclination in any deed whatsoever; and his role in any earthly activities that he does perform will be one of compulsion only.

To attain Humility, Luzzatto urged the disciple to purge his heart before performing a *mitzvah*. Any distracting thoughts should be considered "adultery of the heart" in that they turned the mystic's attention away from his "beloved" toward the vain and deceitful illusions of the world. The six hundred and thirteen *mitzvoth* prescribed by the Torah were sufficient perhaps for the ordinary Jew, but Luzzatto's Kabbalist had to carry them even further. Like the Ari's Cubs, the Circle members also abstained from eating meat or killing even insects—not to mention acting under all circumstances with compassion and mercy toward human beings.

To induce Awe, Luzzatto encouraged the mystic to see himself standing before God, "communicating with Him, even though He cannot be seen." This phase of the preparation for union was hardest because the Kabbalist now had to create a "mental picture" of something he had never seen, where before he had been acting in response to the world of sensory experience. His longing to communicate with God face to face, as with a friend—which would come with the next phase, Love—would impel him to advance from a personal, self-created image of the Absolute, to the impersonal, formless One.

Luzzatto strongly advocated contemplation of one's own grossness and lowliness in the face of the Divine, for Awe resulting from self-abasement, he said, soon transformed itself into Love's yearning. Like an absent lover hearing about his mistress, the Kabbalist woud feel pleasure at the mere mention of God. Saintliness, Humility, and Fear of Sin—all natural components of the mystic's *love* of God—would bring him to *devekuth*, the state of constant union with Him. At this point, he "did not strive for and [was] not concerned with anything outside of Him . . . to the extent that he [could not] separate himself and move from Him." In this state of Holiness, the Kabbalist was ready to contemplate the Psalms of David in ecstatic meditation. The *devekuth* resulting from his efforts was reflected in his constant awareness of God's presence in his sitting, walking, sleeping, and waking life. Luzzatto compared this condition of elevated intimacy with God to the symbol of the tabernacle in the Temple, where the body merely served as a house for the Divine Presence:

> I have already indicated that one cannot accomplish this by himself, but must awaken himself to it and strive for it . . . [with] much separation [from the world], intense contemplation of the secrets of divine governance and the mysteries of Creation, and understanding of the majesty of the Blessed

One . . . to the point where one cleaves closely to Him and is capable of performing physical activities with sacrificial motivation.

In *The Path of the Just*, his chapter-by-chapter outline of the mystic guide to Saintliness, Luzzatto emphasizes "aloneness" above all. Only by shutting out the ephemeral stimuli of the world outside him, he believed, could the Kabbalist learn to recognize the "friend" inside who would teach him the path to God. Beyond that level of *devekuth* lay a realm called "Holy Spirit," where a man was mentally, and sometimes even physically, transformed into a prophet. At this level, like Moses before him, the Kabbalist had entered the "Way of God."

Following the Lurianic Kabbalah, Luzzatto emphasized meditating along the continuum on which the earthly and heavenly human souls exist and meet. He taught his Circle members to contemplate the spheres of the cosmic tree in such a way as to promote "secret movements" from above that would evoke the "inner lights" of each heavenly attribute and turn them toward the supplicating soul below. Then, under the rapt mental direction of the Kabbalist, the "full bliss of the Infinite" would itself flow downward until "all the worlds become conscious of a beneficent influence." Only a man who had reached the stage of Saintliness on the preparatory path, could dare to indulge in this practice which, said Luzzatto, "will turn evil into good."

THE SECRETS OF BETH EL

The last known group of practicing Kabbalists continues to meet today at the Yeshivah Beth El in Jerusalem. Closed to even the most interested observer, the small congregation continues the practices instituted by its predecessors four centuries before. Blending music and silent meditation to induce a state of Awe, the congregants, who, until the early twentieth century, lived communally as a group calling themselves

Mechavenim (those who make prayers with meditation), gathered in a circle at the feet of the *Rav Ha-Hasid* (master of devotion), as he initiated the wordless song that carried them toward ecstasy.

Between the sixteenth and nineteenth centuries, the *Rav Ha-Hasid* acted as the spiritual head not only of the yeshivah, but of Jerusalem and all of Palestine as well. Members of the mystical brotherhood left a document attesting to their spiritually dedicated life style. Each man signed a contract leaving all his worldly and spiritual accomplishments to his fellow congregants—not only in his immediate life, but in all lives to come! Each vowed to sacrifice his life for the others; and each dedicated himself in writing to a single-minded search for nothing less than total union with the Absolute. Some wrote books and manuals designed to guide new members in their meditations; these bear fetching titles like, *The River of Perfection, The Perfume of Joy,* and *Words of Greeting*—yet they remain unintelligible to those who have not been initiated into their secrets by the masters of Beth El.

Ariel Bension, a descendant of one of the members of this community, tells us that it was founded by Spanish-Jewish exiles who were influenced by the Ari's emphasis on the written *kavannot* (concentration symbols) in prayer. The masters at Beth El, says Bension, introduced melodies "to mark the period of meditation." The *Rav Ha-Hasid* sang the meditative melody aloud "to inspire the silent meditation of the *Mechavenim.*" At first it had been the custom to carry on the meditation in deep silences which sometimes lasted for as long as fifteen minutes. But the inspirational melodies gradually replaced the silence, and provided a more ecstatic setting for the contemplative prayer that followed. The master intoned an impromptu, wordless song whose tone and rhythm immediately revealed to the disciples the nature of each particular meditation.

As he led the congregation in the declaration of the *Shema* (the unity of God and His Name), the *Rav Ha-Hasid* simultaneously swept them out of individual consciousness toward union with the *Shekhinah* (God's immanent, female presence). The only requirement for this form of spiritual practice was a yearning heart and an ascetic and prayerful nature. Intellect played little part in the purely devotional contemplation practiced by the Beth El mystics. Three times a day they uttered the same liturgies uttered by Jews all over the world—but their prayer was expressed with a *kavanna* so intense as to evoke the living spirit of God from the sheltering words.

2

Love: The Journey to God

With his soul sufficiently cleansed by the ethical and spiritual
practices centered on Awe, the mystic—now filled with a
lover's yearning for a glimpse of the beloved—is prepared to
reflect a vision of the Absolute. Though it is not yet classified
as "union," this stage, depicted in the erotic imagery of
Solomon's Song of Songs, is a very elevated one. The mystic
no longer feels himself to be a minute, insignificant creature
separated by eons in space and time from his Creator, but
now regards God as his own *dodi* (dear friend). Even at this
exalted level, the lover approaches his goal in stages; the interdependence of the entire chain of worlds along the cosmic
tree allows him to work with Love as he had with Awe, in the
knowledge that God, His idea, and His word are One. Therefore, in the corresponding microcosm of his own mind, the
mystic's thought, speech, and action may also be united as
one. Emptied of his ego, he too is free to create new worlds
with each breath—and to destroy them with each expiration.

The sages in Rabbi Akiva's circle at the Jewish academy of
learning at Yavneh in the first century of the Common Era
employed visualized "journeys" through the spheres to induce
ecstatic states. Designed to further the mystic in his passionate desire to "know" God, these contemplative exercises emphasized mental excursions through heavenly palaces and
elaborate visualizations of God's chariot and throne. In books

like Ezekiel, The Lesser and Greater Hekhalot, Merkabah Rabbah, Shiur Komah, and the Book of Enoch, they outlined this potpourri of Jewish, Persian, and Gnostic meditations so that only the most ardent, most impeccably prepared initiate could practice them. Thus, when Rabbi Akiva warns his younger colleagues not to be fooled by the illusions their minds would inevitably create during these higher states of consciousness, he is telling them only to look at, and not to fall in love with their own projections.

Using the Psalms as a guide book for their visualizations of God's environs, these early mystics embodied ascending grades of consciousness in concrete images that eventually lost their form and merged into pure light. Where earlier they had meditated on God's handiwork expressed in nature and their corporeal selves, they now contemplated the world beyond the senses, beyond even the imagination, until they encountered the very precincts of the Absolute. Thus, the pure marble of God's palace might represent the pure, formless state, the final goal; while water, symbolic of the elements in their primordial state, and falsehood, or ego-inspired illusion, might symbolize the physical and mental traps en route.

WARNINGS TO THE VOYAGER

The author (or authors) of The Lesser Hekhalot (Halls of God's Palace), like Rabbi Akiva, also warns the voyager against the deluding mirages thrown up by the mind:

> The door of the sixth chamber [or level of contemplation] appears like marble covered by a hundred thousand myriad (a billion) waves of water; but it does not have in it even a single drop of water, but rather reflects the glow of the stones of pure marble that are clearly visible in the chamber, and whose luminosity resembles that of water.

Rashi, the great twelfth-century talmudic commentator, elaborates on the first-century text, saying, "Pure marble is as transparent as pure water, but is not, like water, physical or life-producing." Akiva's warning, according to Rashi, is an admonition against the mistaken idea that the mind can take one across the vast gulf dividing matter from spirit. For the mind, too, is composed of the elements; and no physical creation can see God and live. Man must therefore dispense with the mental *idea,* or image, of God and, by transforming himself, *experience* Him.

Sages like Rabbi Hananel ben Chushiel (990–1055 C.E.) prayed, fasted, and went through ritual cleansing procedures before sitting down to contemplate the halls of God's palace. Once there, they "saw" guardian angels, the structure of Ezekiel's worlds within worlds, and even the *Aravot,* a sacred place inhabited by great departed souls. Rabbi Hananel claimed to understand Akiva's warning about these particular contemplation exercises through personal experience: "When you reach that state where you see in the 'stone of the heart' [the heart being the focal point for meditation performed by the 'lover' of God] near the stones of pure marble [the formless state that follows], do not say 'Water! Water!' for there is no water there at all; but only a form is seen. And whoever says 'water,' blasphemes." Rabbi Hananel's meditation nevertheless produced only an imperfect result, for he describes his vision of the Absolute as being reflected through "a speculum that does not shine."

Another eleventh-century sage, Rabbi Nathan ben Yechiel, goes on record as saying that the entire journey merely takes place in the mind of the meditator. By fixing his attention on the *Crown* of the cosmic tree and on the top of his own head, the mystic is enabled to see the halls of God's palace, the angelic hosts, and other higher beings inhabiting that domain of human consciousness. Nor is it merely reflected through a "cloudy speculum." Perhaps aiming his argument at Rabbi Hananel's misty vision, Rabbi Nathan teaches that Akiva's meditation on the "chambers of the heart" (that is, his deep and passionate love of God) produced a perfectly clear picture of His realm—no different from the world as perceived by Akiva's physical eyes.

Rabbi Hai Gaon (939–1038) was more interested in the nature of the man who dared aspire to such a journey. Looking deeply into the Akiva legend, he asked why only Rabbi Akiva emerged whole while others, equally righteous, failed. Answers to such questions, concluded Hai Gaon, could not be found in mere ethics or the Law. He searched the Talmud for precedents, but only found the ancient sages in agreement on the necessity for perfect preparation, both physical and mental. One who wished to perform the ritual had to "fast for a certain number of days and, placing his head between his knees, he whispers to the earth many songs and explicitly uttered praises." Sensory deprivation and trance then resulted in a vision of "seven chambers [which] he will enter one after the next, noting what is in each." Elijah, for example, "went up to the top of [Mount] Carmel, and he bowed himself upon the earth, and he put his face between his knees"—a gesture common among the prophets and a possible means of disorienting the senses quickly. Talmudic sages like Rabbi Chanina ben Dosa used to pray in that position. And Eleazar ben Durdia, a terrible sinner who was reputed to have visited every prostitute in the world, repented by placing his head between his knees and weeping until he died!

Rabbi Hai Gaon advises his readers to stay away from such forms of contemplation until they, like Akiva, have actually experienced divine wisdom: "And God gave Akiva life and all on which he gazed, he thought proper thoughts with proper knowledge." The mystical visions themselves, concludes Rabbi Hai Gaon, are all historically true, successors to a long tradition of visionary transformations experienced by biblical saints and prophets in higher states of consciousness.

Two centuries before Hai Gaon, however, one rebellious voice spoke out against hiding the details of the visionary journey from the common man. Rabbi Shmuel Gaon taught that such "miraculous transformations" were not at all confined to the prophetic experience—but that talmudic legalists had spread this idea around in order to keep ordinary people from practicing these techniques themselves!

A VISION OF THE ABSOLUTE

Essentially centered on two symbols—God's palace and the heavenly chariot, or throne—these "descents"/"ascents" never did become the property of the common man. The mystics who practiced these techniques between 200 B.C. and 200 C.E. were usually scholars who, before they had even begun to practice, were fully conversant with the entire Jewish intellectual and mystical tradition. Moreover, they were perfect adherents to the precepts of the Torah in their daily lives and had attained a level of saintliness that earned them the right to make such a journey at all. From their descriptions of the experience, we learn of a world filled with "fiery living creatures who utter words of praise" and songs which only the perfect initiate may hear without endangering his life.

After passing through seven states of consciousness preceding his first vision of the *hekhalot* (halls of God's palace), the mystic traversed seven further "heavens" before arriving at the Throne of God. The vision usually culminated here with the projected form of a cosmic man poised upon a brilliant seat of glory.

The way was not without obstacles. To pacify the guardians who attempted to bar his path, the sage carried seals containing the names of God which corresponded to His attributes: *Understanding, Judgment, Loving-kindness,* and so on. When he felt himself being distracted by one of the guardians (psychological projections which could manifest in either seductive or horrifying form), the sage visualized the seal and simultaneously pronounced the appropriate name. "Adonai," for example, is the name connected with the attribute of *Judgment;* should the meditator wish to obliterate a frightening image, he merely pictured the sphere of *Judgment* on the cosmic tree in bright red and repeated "Adonai" until the terrifying image disappeared.

In his capacity as a master of the *Merkabah* (Throne mysticism), Rabbi Akiva wrote a number of instruction manuals for inducing ecstasy. These took the form of esoteric readings of the Creation section in Genesis, the Song of Songs, and the Shiur Komah (Measure of the Body). The last book, according to Akiva's alternate reading, prepared the mystic for a vision, first of the *Haluk* (garment of light surrounding God's glory) and then of the glory itself.

A typical *Merkabah* hymn, translated by Dr. Judah Goldin, expresses this ineffable experience of "seeing" God:

> *O wreathed in splendor, crowned with crowns,*
> *O chorister of Him on high,*
> *Extol the Lord enthroned in flames*
> *For in the presence of the Presence,*
> *In the inmost glory*
> *Of the inmost chambers*
> *You set up your posts.*
> *Your names He distinguished from His servants' name,*
> *The flame surrounds, a leaping fire,*
> *Around him burning, glowing coals.*[1]

The ritual called "putting on the Names" literally consisted of clothing oneself in a robe inscribed all over with the sacred Names of God. The *Merkabah* mystic used the external reminder to induce in himself the absolutely undistracted meditation on the Names that would carry him toward visionary experience. Wrapped in his sacred robe—whose features were precisely detailed in another first-century manual, the *Sefer Ha-Malbush* (Book of Clothing)—the mystic was enacting the physical half of a contemplative experience which could not be performed by the mind alone. "Wearing," and there-

[1] Quoted in Gershom Scholem, *Jewish Gnosticism, Merkabah Mysticism, and Talmudic Tradition*, pp. 21–22.

fore embodying, the Names made their recitation all the more powerful.

Let us imagine Rabbi Akiva, having fasted, prayed, and immersed in the ritual bath, now wrapped in his robe of Names, as he ascends the levels of consciousness into the *hekhalot* (halls):

> When I ascended to the first palace I was *hasid* [devout], in the second palace I was *tahor* [pure], in the third *yashar* [sincere], in the fourth I was wholly *tamim* [with God], in the fifth I displayed holiness before God; in the sixth I spoke the *kedushah* [santification] before Him who spoke and created, in order that the guardian angels might not harm me; in the seventh palace I held myself erect with all my might, trembling in all limbs, and spoke the following prayer: "Praise be to Thee who are exalted, praise be to the sublime in the chambers of grandeur."

Akiva emerged from his vision of the Throne of Glory a transformed man. He could now merely look at a person and know whether he was an adulterer or murderer; he assumed mastery over nature; a saint, he was distinguished from all other men by his goodness and his powerful judgment of their deeds.

Rabbi Ishmael, a contemporary of Akiva and himself a master of the *Merkabah* tradition, presented his companions with a list of chants designed to evoke the visionary state of consciousness in which the Throne of Glory appeared. Elaborating on his own experiences, Rabbi Ishmael outlined for his disciples a carefully constructed picture of whom they were to confront, and how they were to react:

> I immediately stood up and gathered the entire great Sanhedrin [rabbinical assembly] and smaller Sanhedrin to the great third foyer in the house of God. I sat on a sofa of pure marble that was given to me by my father Elisha. And there came Rabbi Shimon ben Gamliel, Rabbi Eleazar the Great, Rabbi Eleazar ben Dama . . . Jonathan ben Uziel, Rabbi Akiva, Rabbi Yehudah ben Bava. We came and sat before Him, and

all the masses of companions stood on their feet, for they saw streams of fire and flames of light separating between us and them. And Rabbi Nehuniah ben Hakana sat and arranged before them all the words of the *Merkabah*, its descent and ascent, how one who descends shall do so and how to ascend. When one wishes to descend he would call to Suryah, "the prince of the face," binding him with an oath one hundred-twenty times, using the Name Totrosyai: Totrosyay, Tzurtek, Tutrcyal, Tofgor, Ashruylyay, Zvudial, Vzlterriyal, Tendal, Shuked, Hozya, Yemryon, Vadiryron. One must do this *only* one hundred-twenty times, or he might die. If this is done correctly, he descends immediately and assumes great authority over the *Merkabah*. Dividing the fingers of his hand in the shape used by the High Priest [of the Temple] he utters the Names.

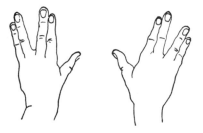

Hand Gestures of High Priests

RABBI NEHUNIAH BEN HAKANA:
APPROACHING THE THRONE OF GOD

Acknowledged by his contemporaries as the greatest expert in the *Merkabah* technique, Rabbi Nehuniah ben Hakana actually directed his companions from within the trance state itself. Surrounding him in awestruck silence, the sages carefully noted down each highly elaborated metaphoric detail of the assault on his senses as he approached the Throne of God.

According to Rabbi Nehuniah, "Totrosyai" was the symbolic guardian of the threshold at the first stage of higher consciousness. Once the mystic had "bound" the guardian by reciting God's appropriate name and visualizing its corresponding attribute, he could continue on without distraction to the next phase. But here, too, he was met by a guardian; eight such "gatekeepers," seated four at each side, would try to interfere with him until he dissolved them with the appropriate chanting and visualization.

Rabbi Nehuniah continues: "The sign and measure of the guardians of the door to the seventh chamber are terrifying, powerful, fearsome . . . sharp swords are in their hands, and flashing lightning emanates from their eyes, and streams of fire from their nostrils, and burning coals from their mouths . . ." Those who entered into the *Merkabah* "without authority" (that is, without proper training by the proper teacher) were grasped and tossed from right to left until they were mentally destroyed or killed. The righteous traveler, on the other hand, was "perfected and illuminated" by the same disorienting experience, the province of Pachdiel, guardian of the fourth chamber. Note that *pachad,* from which this name seems to be derived, is the Hebrew word for "fear." So frightening, then, is the disorienting mental and physical experience of *Merkabah* meditation that a man might die in the attempt. Rabbi Nehuniah therefore warns his companions to "gaze and look and listen, and write all that I say . . . from before the Throne of Glory . . . be careful that you choose . . . proper individuals who have been screened."

From the midst of his trance, he next recounts being buffeted by a "storm wind," an encompassing mass of air that tries to suffocate him. The wind is followed by a levitation experience, during which the master is lifted into a "chariot of brightness," accompanied by trumpets resembling the sound of "eighty million horns and thirty million *shofars,* and forty million bugles" (all probably derived from altered breathing patterns, lack of external stimuli, and intense concentration). Now Rabbi Nehuniah finds himself being grabbed and shaken by the guardian Katzpiel, but because he has mastered the entire Torah and canons of Jewish Law, he is flung loose at the intercession of Gabriel, who quiets the other guardians and brings Rabbi Nehuniah closer to the Throne. The tormentors sheathe their weapons; the assault is apparently ended. But, to be on the safe side, Rabbi Nehuniah describes himself flashing the visualizations of God's Name and mystic signs before them again. Subdued at last, the terrible guardians part from him, leaving Rabbi Nehuniah to enter a hall where he is entertained by the calming music of the heavenly spheres. Spiritually refreshed, he continues into the seventh chamber, where he gazes into the flaming eyes of the *Chayot,* highly vibrating living beings composed of pure energy, and the wheel-shaped *Ofanim,* winged eyes that glitter with the inherent brilliance of God's presence, the *Shekhinah.*

The sight is so overwhelming that Rabbi Nehuniah "trembles and shakes and shudders and is stricken and faints and falls backward." Feeling he can go no further, Rabbi Nehuniah draws himself up and chants as loud as he can:

> *Melech avir, melech adir, melech adon,*
> *Melech baruch, melech bachur, melech baruk,*
> *Melech gadol, melech gibor, melech gaavah.* . . .

an alphabetical series of praises to his "King of Air," "Blessedness," "Greatness," "Power," and so on. The sound of his chanting evokes a vision of friendly angels, who urge him on, saying: "Do not fear. Come in and see the King in His beauty. You will not be destroyed. You will not be burned." And suddenly, almost before he realizes it, Rabbi Nehuniah finds himself before the coveted Throne of Glory.

Even at this supernal peak of contemplation, however, the mystic is tortured by illusory personifications of the flesh: iron axes chip away at him, he is overcome by successive waves of hot and cold water, the guardians buzz around, trying to deafen him, yet he must continue to fix his heart and mind on the image of the Throne, ignoring all else, even if he were to die on the spot.

Returning from his blissful "journey," Rabbi Nehuniah continued his discourses, elaborating the fine points in normal consciousness.

Rabbi Nehuniah ben Hakana's legends and teachings flourished long after his death—but in secret, for at the end of the talmudic period his immediate circle dwindled, leaving only a few initiates to pass down second hand the techniques he had illustrated so vividly.

THE BOOK OF LIGHT

Then, eleven centuries later, in Provence, there suddenly appeared a book which purported to reveal those teachings once again. According to its anonymous compiler, the text of the *Bahir* (Book of Light) is composed of the very discourses given by Rabbi Nehuniah ben Hakana in trance. Many scholars regard the alleged "discourses" as an interesting twelfth-century fabrication of a first-century manuscript. If this is true, then the author of the *Bahir* must be regarded as a great *Merkabah* master in his own right! Using simple, epigrammatic instruction, the "Rabbi Nehuniah" of the *Bahir* led his pupils from the point of spiritual curiosity, through Awe, Love, and yearning, to the Throne itself:

"People want to see the King, but they don't even know where His house is. So they must ask first, 'Where is the King's abode?' Once they have done this they may begin to look for the King Himself." In this homely fashion, the master of the *Bahir* directed the disciple to look within, "for it is the heart of the disciple that the 'King' inhabits."

Building on the metaphor, the master depicts Nature as the King's emissary, His medium, through which He projects Himself (in humble disguise) into this world. Human thought, also part of Nature, is man's emissary. Insofar as it has no end, man may extend himself through thought—all the way to the end of the world—to confront God. Since all of man's sensory faculties were no more than extensions of thought, the imaginative faculty was the source and ruler of all created things. Gazing into the Throne of Glory only meant descending into oneself in order to *ascend* to the Infinite: "For one can arrive at the limit of a person's knowledge, but not at the limit of his thought."

REVEALING THE COSMIC BODY

Another form of ecstatic contemplation attributed to the first-century sages was designed to reveal to the perfect initiate the secret byways of the cosmic body. Those who reached the level of the Throne reported seeing the outline of a *man,* for man had literally been created in the image of God. Given the "face" and "beard" of *Adam Kadmon,* the great cosmic reflection of the body of God, the mystic was directed to imagine himself journeying along nine paths within the beard of the immense, glowing countenance, the anthropomorphic vision of the formless Absolute. When he lost himself among the symmetrical hairs of the beard, the mystic was believed to have grown "mighty and strong" in the art of contemplation.

Once the devotee had united himself with the Divine Image, he, like God, obtained dominion over the sensory world. Like Moses, he could dry up the sea; and like Joshua, Moses' protégé, he could hold back the sun. The power over men's fortunes, believed to lie in the "oil" of the beard, also fell to his lot. "Those who have mastered the difficult techniques of mystical prayer and devout *kavanna* can . . . sometimes channel the flow of [good] fortune to those places and persons that stand in need of it," says the author of *The Body of God,* another anonymous medieval text which claims ancient origins. Manipulating the "holy fortune" residing within the "oil" of God's "beard" is an elaborate metaphor for the powers of the saint whose selfless devotion had removed him from the limits of space and time. Moses, whose meditations

45

had risen to the ninth level of the cosmic "beard," was so spiritually evolved that "he could bring light for all, and judgment would disappear." In practical terms, this meant that he could suspend the course of temporal affairs to benefit the nation he loved so deeply.

To perform such exalted feats, it was imperative that the mystic expand the divine spark lodged within his own soul. The *neshamah,* indestructible, brilliant, unmoved by earthly cares, was his immediate link to God. Although "the Ancient One is recondite and unknown . . . with the emergence of the Father, one can speak of a 'beginning,' and from this point forward man can learn something of him," concludes the author of *The Body of God.* Only the *neshamah,* that portion of God implanted in man, could lead the mystic to an understanding of the divine paradoxes: that we are both separate from God, yet part of Him; that He is within and without, formed, but not formed. In meditating on the nine "lights," "spheres," or "channels" of the beard, the pure soul would inevitably find that the nine apparently separate qualities had merely been reflections of the One all along: "So too is the Holy Ancient One. He is the Supernal Lamp, the Most Concealed. He is not discoverable, except for the rays of light that come forth which are both revealed and hidden . . . *thus all things are one."* (Italics mine.)

The accessible "Father," or small countenance of the cosmic man, was the "you" to whom the lover addressed his immediate, personal communication. "He," the Ancient One, undisclosed, was called "the Father of all other fathers." For the Jewish mystic who contemplated God's countenance in the form of the cosmic man, God's Torah emerged as a magnificent female consisting of seventy faces beneath which there lived a soul wrapped in beautiful garments and wearing a crown. Thus, the "Father" and "Mother" of the universe—God and His *Shekhinah*—enact the cosmic drama on the stage of the devotee's *neshamah,* the divine portion of his human soul. The

"Father" and "Mother" were therefore always depicted in kabbalistic meditation as lovers, united face to face within the sphere of the Infinite.

THE FEMALE ASPECT OF GOD

A favorite subject for meditation among medieval Spanish Kabbalists, the *Matrona,* or female aspect of God's face, negates the charge that Jewish mysticism has no room for woman. Since the very presence of the living God in the world is female, the *Shekhinah/Matrona,* lodged in the sphere of *Sovereignty* on the cosmic tree, is the most accessible part of the Divine Body.

Rabbi Joseph, a thirteenth-century mystic, writes in his *Sefer Tashak:* "She so pervades this lower world that if you search in deed, speech, thought, and speculation, you will find *Shekhinah,* for there is no beginning nor end to her."[2] In her gentle aspect she is the attribute of *Understanding* on the cosmic tree of life, the wise Mother. Spurned by her children and cut off from her Lord, she is *Judgment,* red with anger. In the Kabbalist's visualization, her hair, like the Father's beard, is black, oiled, and curly: "In each tress hang many strands, and each strand illumines many worlds." Her hair is alive with the power of destruction; her cheeks are like luminous red apples. When provoked, the beauteous Mother is fierce.

Rabbi Joseph's erotic motif presents the cosmos in the form of a grand sexual embrace. In his meditations, the King and Queen of the universe are united, "the fingers of their hands are intertwined, forming a circle in which dwell the souls of the righteous and the holy angels."[3] Rabbi Joseph saw each sphere on the tree as a "limb" of the cosmic body, and the Torah as the key to the entire anatomical structure. Thus, he

[2] I am grateful to Professor Jeremy Zwelling of Wesleyan University for furnishing me with this original material.
[3] Compare this graphically erotic motif with Indian artistic representation of Siva and Sakti in sexual embrace.

could visualize the very shapes of the letters inscribed in the Torah scrolls as a sexual embrace between God and *She-khinah*. In his unique and ingenious system, the Hebrew letter *yod* (י), sign of circumcision, became the phallus of the King; the letter *zayin* (ז), an extended *yod*, the phallus as it was about to be received by the letter *chet* (ח), which Rabbi Joseph urged his disciples to visualize as "the *Matrona* whose legs are spread to receive the *zayin*"(!). Since all human activity has its divine counterpart, he argued, the Kabbalist's selfless "reunification" efforts on earth would restore wholeness to the universe.

PASSIONATE SEEKERS AFTER GOD

At the other extreme sat the medieval German Hasidim. In rebellion against the inevitable temptations of the body, these ascetics expressed their Love for God by rolling naked in the snow and, cutting holes in the ice, immersing themselves in the subzero water. In summer (if they survived their winter mortifications) they smeared their naked bodies with honey and exposed themselves to swarms of bees. An unsympathetic contemporary describes their antics thus:

> They set themselves up as prophets by practicing the pronunciation of holy names, or sometimes they only direct their intention upon them without actually pronouncing the words. Then a man is seized by terror and his body sinks to the ground. The barrier in front of his soul falls, he himself steps into the center and gazes into the faraway, and only after a while, when the power of the name recedes, does he awaken and return with a confused mind to his former state.[4]

Like all other lovers, passionate seekers after God vary greatly. Most impressive perhaps is the apocalyptic legend of Enoch, whose unfailing righteousness results in the highest vision of the Throne and heavenly hosts and ends with the

[4] Quoted in Gershom Scholem, *Major Trends in Jewish Mysticism*, p. 102.

transformation of a flesh-and-blood mystic into an angelic superman. In Enoch we see the Jewish mystic at his ideal best, having developed from the lowest *madregot* (levels) of observation and self-reckoning to holiness and ultimate perfection. The Book of Enoch is believed to have been written by a group of first-century devotees who inscribed their practices for posterity under the cloak of a wondrous fable. Enoch, the grandfather of Noah, first presented as an observer of nature in its minutest details, is a man so personally integrated with the seasonal cycles that he is entirely unafraid of death. Having immersed himself in the Creation, he functions in perfect accord with the commandments—to the extent that he attains perceptions beyond the range of ordinary human beings.

Following the Jewish mystic pattern to perfection, he graduates from the social to the hermitic way of life, where solitude and prayer open his inner eye to the world of angelic beings. Soon Enoch is able to commute with ease between the world of men and the heavenly realm of angels. Functioning as a divine messenger, he exhorts mankind to turn away from its worldly preoccupations toward spiritual ones, while his highly developed psychic abilities enable him to learn the divine mysteries directly from the lips of the angels.

Like Rabbi Nehuniah ben Hakana, Enoch too makes various contemplative "journeys" of ascent and descent and also describes to a recorder the physical details of his visions. Enumerating each of the five senses through an intricate set of metaphors, he climbs high mountains, fords crystal streams, and wanders through heavenly halls on his "eastward" voyage. In one nameless country of the mind he finds nothing but aromatic plants and herbs, a land of fragrant scents. In the "north," like Nehuniah, Enoch too is met, but not overcome, by an unearthly onslaught of storm and wind. (Perhaps the result of meditating on the *Crown* of the head.) His "wandering" at an end, he enters the chambers of the heavenly palace, whose occupants, the first order of angels, teach him astronomical secrets and introduce him to the divine attribute of

Understanding, personified by a female on a royal throne. Exploring still further, he encounters the "small countenance" of God:

> *And there I saw One, who had a head of days,*
> *And His head was white like wool,*
> *And with Him was another being whose countenance*
> *   had the appearance of a man [Messiah],*
> *And his face was full of graciousness, like one*
> *   of the holy angels.*

But Enoch is destined for still greater heights of awareness. Passing over seven mountains composed of seven different metals, he enters a valley inhabited by avenging angels. Yet even these avengers are easily tamed by his saintliness, and they teach him the secrets of lightning and thunder before guiding him forward. At last, in the five hundredth year, seventh month, and fourteenth day of Enoch's life, he comes face to face with the Ancient of Days on His Throne—the final vision attainable by a mortal human being. Immediately, Enoch is transported live to heaven and transformed into the angel Metatron.

And from that day I was no longer numbered amongst
[men]; and [an angel] set me between the two winds, between
the north and the west, where the angels took the cords
to measure for me the place for the elect and righteous.

Surrounded by the blessed sons of God whose faces and garments are so white and radiant that they nearly blind him and cause him to fall on his face, Enoch is next seized by the angel Michael, who lifts him still higher while disclosing to him all the secrets of the seven heavens.

At the final vision of the Ancient of Days, surrounded by ten times ten thousands of *Seraphim*, *Cherubim*, and *Ofanim*, purified by crystal tongues of living fire, Enoch falls upon his face.

And my whole body became relaxed,
And my spirit was transfigured;
And I cried with a loud voice . . .

With the transformation of Enoch in the face of the Almighty, Jewish mysticism reaches that immeasurable peak of spiritual Love which marks the journey's end in a place where human speech cannot follow.

II
Kabbalistic Practices

3

The Path of Spheres

Since the Middle Ages the cosmic tree of life with its ten spheres, or divine attributes, has been the central image of kabbalistic meditation. Though some masters adapted the "seven heavens" of the first-century *Merkabah* mystics, equating them with the seven lower branches of the tree, most Kabbalists focused their attention on the symbolic tree alone. With its inner "lights," corresponding colors, metals, and divine names, the tree itself was complicated enough. The mystic's attitude as he approached meditation on the spheres proved him to be as certain of his ultimate goal as he was reverential. Says Moses de Leon, a thirteenth-century Spanish Kabbalist:

> When God gave the Torah to Israel, He opened the seven heavens to them, and they saw that nothing was there in reality but His Glory; He opened the seven worlds to them and they saw that nothing was there but His Glory; He opened the seven abysses before their eyes, and they saw that nothing was there but His Glory. Meditate on these things and you will understand that God's essence is linked and connected with all worlds, and that all forms of existence are linked and connected with each other, but derived from His existence and essence.[1]

[1] Quoted in Gershom Scholem, *Major Trends in Jewish Mysticism*, p. 223.

In this spirit, the mystic prepared to scale the tree, confront the worlds, acknowledge the links through his own person, and come to a direct experience of the divine ground on which the whole scheme rests.

The sphere of *Sovereignty* represents our world of matter. *Foundation, Endurance,* and *Majesty* combine as the premanifest world of spirit. *Beauty, Loving-kindness,* and *Judgment* form the world of creation. While the world of *Wisdom, Understanding,* and *Crown* is the very domain of divine immanence. Thus, in "climbing" mentally toward his source, the mystic traverses the myriad universes embodied in the ten spheres, as well as the four archetypal worlds, the seventy divine names, and innumerable "faces" on the tree. The culmination of all devotional, contemplative, and visionary works alluding to this ascent—the guide book of guide books—is the *Zohar,* or "Book of Splendor." A massive compendium of stories and biblical exegesis, this book both decoded the esoteric Torah and presented the devotee with a detailed map of the visionary landscape he would be exploring along the tree. "When I open the book *Zohar*," said the Baal Shem Tov, "I behold the whole universe." And he meant it literally.

RABBI SIMEON BAR YOHAI AND THE "ZOHAR"

Scholars, on the other hand, call the *Zohar* a brilliant forgery devised by Moses de Leon, who, they say, attributed the work to the great Tannaitic sages in an attempt to legitimize it. Forgery or no, the *Zohar* is indispensable to an understanding of Jewish mystical life from the Middle Ages to our own times. The background of the book is well known: Rabbi Simeon bar Yohai, its hero, was a second-century sage who, accompanied by his son Eleazar, lived in a cave for thirteen years to escape the Romans who had killed his master, Rabbi Akiva. Miraculously sustained by a carob tree and a fountain, which both sprang up at the mouth of their cave, the father and son sat buried in sand all day in order to protect themselves from the scorching sun that shines on the area that is now occupied by the Ben-Gurion Airport in Lod (Lydda), Israel. Here they studied the Torah under the guidance of the prophet Elijah. In the thirteenth year of their exile, the Roman emperor Trajan, their principal persecutor, died, leaving the two sages free to emerge from hiding. Horrified at the lack of spirituality he encountered among the Jews on his return, Rabbi Simeon returned to his cave to meditate for another year. At the end of that period a voice resounded through the cave, urging him to leave ordinary men to their own devices and to teach only those who were ready to hear him. The discourses given by Rabbi Simeon at the urging of that divine order—recorded by the loyal group of "companions" who gathered round him on his second re-emergence into the world—comprise the *Zohar*.

Rabbi Simeon bar Yohai apparently belonged to that small group of gifted teachers whose mere presence could transform spiritually any man, woman, child, or animal. He taught that all observable things here were reflected in a higher world and that no thing or person survived independently on any plane of existence, no matter how high. Anyone determined to elevate his own soul was therefore automatically committing himself to elevate every sentient, and even insentient, entity in God's creation. "All souls form but one unity with the Divine Soul," was the basis for all his teachings. The entire aim of a man's stay on earth, said Rabbi Simeon, is to realize this in the experience of union:

> All things of which this world is composed, as the soul and the body, will return to the principle and to the root from which they sprang. For God is the beginning and He is the end of all the degrees of creation. And all the degrees are bound with His seal. He is the unique Being, in spite of the innumerable forms in which He is clothed.

Rabbi Simeon's message is therefore a call to union with the Divine. In his view even the written and spoken Torah are actually One, since they emerge directly from the revelation at Sinai, where God's words were each divided into seventy sounds which appeared in the form of seventy lights that enabled the Israelites to *see* the words as they *heard* them. Similarly, the spheres, also emanations from the One, provide the Kabbalist with the opportunity to relive the Sinai mystery in his meditations. More than mere rungs on a ladder, the divine attributes actualize the otherwise physically imperceptible notion of God. So closely intertwined are these attributes with the very words of the Torah that they are virtually interchangeable for purposes of contemplation. When seen in this light, the divine attributes (which are themselved interchangeable) resound with the hidden Names which God assigned to Himself.

The Cosmic Tree with Divine Names

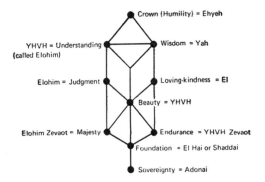

The egoless heart of the mystic radiates these illumined names and is simultaneously absorbed by them. Rabbi Simeon taught many forms of meditation on the spheres. One example of the multiple possibilities he expounded was to imagine the attributes as a series of dancing lights against the branches of the tree. Closing his eyes, the Kabbalist visualized them vibrating with color, blazing with the letters of the divine names, each one reflecting its corresponding metal, planet, angel, and human body part. He gazed until the lights began to shift positions; one mounting on the left; one descending on the right; one entering between them. Two spheres crown themselves with a third; three merge into one; one suddenly emanates many colors. Then six spheres descend all at once, doubling to twelve. Twelve become twenty-two, then six again, and then ten. At last, all the spheres are swallowed up in one.

Although there is a definite resemblance between this mental exercise and certain drug-induced experiences of light, color, and movement, we ought not assume that Rabbi Simeon and his companions were transporting themselves with hallucinogens. All evidence points to a strict pattern of mental concentration in an alert state heightened by nothing more than fasting, perhaps, and isolation.

The parts of the Kabbalist's body, too, are alive with knowledge. The seven lower spheres on the tree correspond to seven centers of heavenly power disbursed along the spine. Meditation on the spine reveals that a human being is composed of male (active, fiery) energy on the right, and female (receptive, watery) on the left. Thus, says Rabbi Simeon, in observing and combining the two qualities, the disciple actually experiences the unifying principle of creation directly: "In the form of God He made him, male and female He made them" (Genesis 1:27). Furthermore, the seven lower spheres by which the transcendent Absolute is comprehensible to man all share human neural counterparts which, like the spheres along the tree, meet in the highest center located in the brain. Rabbi Simeon refers metaphorically to the crown of the head as "the Brooks of God," and, reminding his companions of The Song of Songs, asks: "What is this 'fountain of gardens, a well of living waters, flowing from Lebanon'? It is nothing more than the sphere representing *Wisdom*." And since the word "Lebanon" comes from the same root as *laban*, "white," Solomon also here means it to represent the "white matter in the brain." In Rabbi

Simeon's hands, the entire verse becomes an esoteric lesson in contemplation:

> Come with me from Lebanon, bride, with me
> from Lebanon! Look from the top of Amana,
> from the top of Senir and Hermon, from
> the lion's dens, from the mountains of the leopards.

Breath and sound emerge from the white matter in the human brain, here called "Lebanon." "Amana" is the throat, which projects the breath from the topmost nerve center of the body and allows it to circulate downward to the lower nerve centers along the spine. The top of "Senir" and "Hermon" represent the tongue; the "lion's den," the teeth; the "mountains of the leopards," the lips and speech.

KING SOLOMON'S BREATHING EXERCISE

Solomon, gifted in speech and song, devised this contemplative exercise, says Rabbi Simeon, as a result of his own ecstatic experiences. Having attained to the seventh sphere on the tree, he condensed the mystic ascent into three books for those who would follow. The Song of Songs therefore represents the nature of the sphere known as *Beauty;* Ecclesiastes depicts the sphere of *Judgment;* and Proverbs characterizes *Loving-kindness.* Solomon's father David, also a poet, transmitted to him the technique for evoking the "holy breath," or inspiration, which induced the visionary experiences and, ultimately, the three great books. Says Rabbi Simeon, "the human breath is a mixture of subtle elements comprised of air, fire, and water. Without breath we die. By learning and practicing the secrets inherent in the breath, Solomon could lift nature's physical veil from created things and see the spirit within." What is usually translated in Ecclesiastes as "vanity" (*hebli*) may therefore be read esoterically as: "I have seen all things in the days of my *breath, hebel.*" In some as yet undisclosed way, Rabbi Simeon taught Solomon's technique of directing attention to the white matter in the brain while altering normal breathing patterns. Insisting that union between man and God "is best effected on earth" through the vehicle of breath, he likened the mystery of breathing to the sacred *Shema,* the daily declaration of God's unity with His Name. Rabbi Simeon pointed out that the three names contained in the blessing— YHVH, *Elohaynu,* YHVH—signify the fire, air, and water of the human breath. Visualizing the three highest attributes on the tree (*Crown, Wisdom,* and *Understanding*) as he recites the declaration, the Kabbalist makes of his own breath a channel for the divine influx. "Whilst a man's mouth and lips are moving his heart and will must soar to the height of heights, so as to acknowledge the unity of the whole."

MEDITATION ON THE "SHEMA"

The first word, *"Shema"* (Hear), also contains the word *shem* (name). Composed of six words, the phrase stands for the six created directions and their unification in the One Name. The second word, "Israel," is a euphemism for the attribute *Beauty* and the patriarch Jacob. By singing "Hear, O Israel!" the Kabbalist effects a unification between *Beauty* and *Sovereignty,* the spiritual Israel with the earthly one. The following four words, "YHVH" (Lord), *"Elohaynu"* (our God), "YHVH" (Lord), and *"Echad"* (One), state that God is both the many and the One. This "mystery of Faith" affirms the completeness of the Name and its attributes. YHVH and His creation are one; the oral and written Torah are one; His emblems are interchangeable with His names; the "higher" world and the "lower" world symbolically unite as the recitation is sung, and the mind avows the unity of the spheres.

The Kabbalist concentrates the whole idea of unification in the word *echad* (one) by dwelling twice as long on this word and so emphasizing its last letter, *d,* fourth letter of the Hebrew alphabet and synonymous with the sphere of *Judgment.* By dwelling on that sphere, says Rabbi Simeon, a man comes to see how small he actually is when compared to the Divine One.

The concluding verse following the *Shema* ("Blessed be the Name of the glory of His kingdom forever and ever"), also six words in Hebrew, harmonizes the six created directions in the lower world of *Sovereignty:* "For our Master has taught us that the 'Hear, O Israel' and the 'Blessed be the Name' are a summary of the whole Torah." Since they also symbolize male and female energies respectively, the two phrases, when uttered in perfect harmony of mind, breath, and body, unify spirit and nature.

Another way of meditating on the all-important body centers was to visualize the spinal column as the *lulav* (palm branch) and the heart as the *etrog* (citron)—ritual objects used during the Feast of Tabernacles at the harvest season. Regarding his body as the Tabernacle containing the Divine Spirit, the Kabbalist meditated on the fragrant-smelling citron, visualizing it at his heart's core. The single pillar extending from heaven to earth which led the Israelites through the wilderness became synonymous in his mind with the *lulav* visualized as his spine.

Rabbi Simeon bar Yohai couched his entire message in similar allegories, digressions, and elaborate esoteric analyses of biblical story and ritual custom. Indeed, the *Zohar* might be called the "encyclopedia" of Jewish mysticism for its diversity and fullness. The first discourse, for example, opens with a geometric analogy sketching the four archetypal worlds on the cosmic tree as four interlocking triangles, and ends on a totally different note. Since it is inhabited by the least accessible attributes of *Crown, Wisdom,* and *Understanding,* the highest world can only be represented by a primordial point in space. This point, the topmost part of the Hebrew letter *yod,* is the beginning of the sacred name. *Wisdom* is depicted by a circle, *Understanding* by a square. By gazing at these geometric designs and contemplating them as divine "attributes," the Kabbalist, says Rabbi Simeon, is sanctifying God in space. In this context, with a logic all its own, the *Zohar* devotes an entire portion to the story of Abraham, who, says Rabbi Simeon, portrays the interdependence between human effort and divine impulse better than any other biblical figure.

ABRAHAM'S SPIRITUAL JOURNEY

When Abraham moved "toward the Holy Land and away from Haran," he was actually aspiring toward the spiritual life. Moreover, he took a whole company of souls with him, thereby doubling the effect of his own effort, "since one who puts another in the path of righteousness ever reaps benefit from his merit also." As a result of their own previous incarnations, the good souls "made in Haran" were permitted to accompany him. The prototype for all aspirants to divine *Wisdom*, Abraham first had to descend into "Egypt" (the material world of desire, ego, ambition), probing the depths of worldly experience before scaling the tree. Unlike Adam, who took *Wisdom* precipitately, or Noah, who grew drunk with it, Abraham was the first dweller in the pit of worldliness to merit it when he emerged. Firmly yoked in his mind and heart to the sphere of *Wisdom*, he was not distracted from his purpose, even when Egypt, "the land of the magicians," lured him with its promise of luxury and supernatural power. "There he preserved himself from being seduced by those bright essences, and, after testing himself, he returned to his place: he 'went up' from Egypt literally, strengthened and confirmed in faith, and reached the highest grade of faith."

Abraham's arduous spiritual journey, detailed in the exoteric tales of his wanderings and testing by God, ended when he reached the level of illumination called *Wisdom*. To designate his achievement, a letter of God's name was added to his, and Abram became Abraham. His entry into the Holy Land corresponded to his "building an altar" in each sphere along the way—that is, leaving part of himself behind in every one of them until he was sufficiently empty to be filled by *Wisdom*.

In imitation of Abraham, says Rabbi Simeon,\
must prepare to traverse the spheres by stabilizi\
cal elements within himself. Only the perfectly te\
could survive the symbolic tests of faith endured l\
Where the first patriarch stood for *Wisdom*, in tl   -,
his son Isaac, having withstood the supreme sacrificial test,
came to embody *Judgment*. Jacob, the "prudent" patriarch,
was the symbol of *Beauty*. In the same manner, each patriar-
chal sphere could be contemplated as a specific limb of the
cosmic body, a letter or sound of the holy Name, a color, a
light, a geometric form, and so on. Even the priestly sacrifices in the Temple could stand as emblems for contemplation.

The smell of incense surrounding the sacrificial altar caused
an inward contraction of the nose which pervaded the brain,
stilled the thoughts, and produced a "pleasing sensation."
Contrary to the ordinary reading of Deuteronomy, Rabbi
Simeon's interpretation of the "savor of appeasement" does
not refer to burnt offerings which placate an irate and perpet-
ually angry God, but rather views the "incense" as an aid in
reducing one's own "anger" and restoring calm to the agitated
human mind, permitting bliss and illumination to enter. The
smoke rising from the symbolic altar of the temple of the
body therefore condenses "the fires of anger until a reunion is
formed, an appeasement of the spirit, a universal rejoicing, a
radiance of lamps, a brightening of faces."

The daily offering of a certain libation of wine on the Temple altar was really the joyful spirit of the mystic as he
approached his meditative prayer. The process of "lighting the
lamps" meant illuminating the spark of *neshamah* within oneself in order to bring down the heavenly light. The word "Israel" meant the human heart; "Holy Land" was the state of
enlightenment or *devekuth;* and "Egypt" the distracting poi-
son of the sense world. Even the building of the Temple was
analogous to expanding the spirit within the body. To this
end, Rabbi Simeon expounded on the perennial "spirit of life"

hich is "exhaled" by God and then gathered by man in the throat. In a state of perfect concentration, man may consciously accumulate the "spirit of life" and convert it into holy energy, *Elohim Hayim*, "the living God." At this point the divine energy compels the earth, air, fire, and water of the body to return to their simplest state, thereby reducing thought to pure sound. In this suspended condition, the body and mind are so still that the Kabbalist has become a hollow channel vibrating with divine energy. This stage, called "the House is being built," indicates that he has transcended the limited perceptions imposed on man by thought. The carefully elaborated plans and materials for the great Temple of Solomon were thus transformed by Rabbi Simeon into an inspiring mental exercise by which a man could envision his own perfection.

Moses, "a Master of the House," had so entirely stilled his thoughts and purified his body that he instantly perceived and adhered to God (*Crown*). Jacob, on the other hand, could not fully detach himself from his anxieties about his earthly family and so reached a lower degree of illumination (*Beauty*). Conversely, those who suffered from the effects of a diffuse and impure mind merely constructed for themseves a "Tower of Babel."

More than an intellectual game or religious acrostic, the *Zohar* emphasizes over and over again the unity of word, thought, and energy. To link oneself in higher states of consciousness to the *sound* of holiness (as, for example, in reciting the *Shema*) was in fact to link oneself to its essence. The emblematic tales of the patriarchs, like the spheres they represent, could be further reduced to the very letters of God's Name. Rabbi Simeon's map of consciousness reaches even beyond the sphere of *Wisdom* and embraces all creation:

> Truly all that God does in the world is an emblem of the divine Wisdom . . . Further, all the works of God are the ways of the Torah . . . and no single word is contained in it but is

an indication of ever so many ways and paths ar
divine Wisdom . . . Each incident recorded in the
tains a multitude of deep significations, and each word i
an expression of Wisdom and the doctrine of truth.

Since the entire created universe—as presented through the
divine attributes on the tree—could at any point provide the
Kabbalist with a meditative key, his means were as complex
and innumerable as the myriad created things around and
inside him. What could he expect to see when he commenced
his ascent from diversity toward the unity encompassed by
the first mystic point of the letter *yod* within the sphere of
the *Crown?* Rabbi Simeon told him that in deep contemplation the spheres reveal themselves to be contained one
within the other like the skins of an onion, "brain within brain
and spirit within spirit, so that one is a shell to another." What
earlier masters of the *Merkabah* called *hekhalot*, or "halls of
God's palace," were, he said, actually extensions of the primal
point at the *Crown* which cannot be comprehended by human
reason. The so-called "palace" functions as a protective garment for this primal light, lessening its brilliance so that
human beings may comprehend it. The first "hall" encompasses another, the second, still another, and so on, each
descending "hall" creating a membrane of sorts for the one
preceding it. To prepare himself for the ultimate light, the
Kabbalist "studies" the Torah—that is, contemplates its letters
in a state of ecstasy.

"When praying," says Rabbi Simeon, "I raise my hand on
high, that when my mind is concentrated on the highest, there
is higher still that which can never be known or grasped, the
starting point that is absolutely concealed, that produced what
it produced while remaining unknowable, and irradiated what
it irradiated while remaining undisclosed."

Next, he attempted to visualize the first emanation of that
point of light. This detached "fragment of the Absolute"
would become the first of the humanly comprehensible "halls"
—the sphere of *Wisdom.* The strain of concentrating at this

high level, however, would be too great if the light did not dim sightly. This is the function of the second membrane, or "hall", the sphere called *Understanding*. From here there issue forth still less subtle fragments of the original light, which Rabbi Simeon advises using as a ladder for yet another contemplative ascent toward *Crown*. So much for the visualization aspect of the exercise.

Besides sitting with his head between his knees in the traditional meditation posture, we may ask what else Rabbi Simeon was doing and thus try to piece together some organized technique from the deliberately scrambled text. Perhaps a lesson in breathing given by Rabbi Eleazar, his son, provides another clue. Emulating Ezekiel, Eleazar enjoins his "companions" to produce the contemplative impulse on earth in order to stimulate a response from above. At first he "exhorts the winds to come from all four directions and fill his breath." This, says Rabbi Eleazar, means to circulate the air inhaled from "all four directions interchangeably, understanding that the western direction in particular will issue spirits that take human form. [A warning about hallucination that might result from hyperventilation?] Breathe in the same way that the sea takes and gives, and therefore is not full."

The densely metaphorical language of the *Zohar* prohibits further attempts at piecing together the step-by-step procedure for kabbalistic meditation on the tree of spheres. In all my discussions with contemporary Kabbalists, I have yet to come across a clear and practical set of instructions. The *Zohar*'s thirteenth-century contemplative techniques gave way to the sixteenth-century *yichudim* (binding of the spheres) of the Ari, Isaac Luria, and finally melted into obscurity with the decline of the nineteenth-century Hasidic movement.

BINDING OF THE SPHERES

The Ari's *yichudim* aimed at nothing less than unifying the name of God with its source in the sphere of the *Crown*. Only the elect could practice the *yichud,* for it demanded an unfaltering commitment to redeeming the world as one liberated oneself. The colors of the spheres, said the Ari, were not "colors" in the physical sense, but rather symbols of the qualities represented by each sphere. Red, for example, stood for *Judgment* because human beings ascribe the color of blood to anger. All red things in nature, then, are derived from the energy inherent in the attribute called *Judgment.* White stands for *Loving-kindness,* for compassion usually brings that color to mind. The spiritual world is personified by color in order to aid the meditator's imagination. When the Ari wished to transmit mercy toward someone, he visualized *Loving-kindness* in white, as the Temple priests had done to evoke that particular attribute on the Day of Atonement. To the visualized sphere he added an appropriate angelic name, pronounced while holding the breath and moving only the larynx and tongue—a technique called "swallowing."

The crucial point for the Kabbalist performing the *yichud* occurred at the stage of "reversal," when he had "climbed" as far along the tree as he could and, having drawn the light from the highest sphere attained, he descended with it toward the physical world once again. This reversal of the divine flow, which made it possible for even the lowest creatures in the lowest world to absorb the light of the Infinite, required more than an ordinary share of purity, mental strength, and humility. The Ari felt that even the good men of Safed were not really equal to the task of pacifying the terrible guardians of the spheres encountered by their predecessors, the Tannaitic sages. Because of this, he encouraged his disciples to concentrate instead on those specific spheres on the tree from which their own souls had sprung. If the Kabbalist was truly saintly, then he would evoke the assistance of a "good angel," or the soul of a departed saint who shared the same soul root as he. Having bound his soul to each attribute in turn and reached the highest point on the tree, the Kabbalist would experience a tremendous influx of light. Certain individuals recorded apprehending the light in the form of an angel. Samuel, for example, characterized it thus: "The spirit of God spoke in me, and His word was on my tongue" (2 Samuel 23:2). Sometimes a man was so stunned by the shock of the light traveling through his body that he fell back, trembling all over, or even fainting. His ultimate aim was to "reach" the Quarry of Souls at the highest point on the tree and, meeting the source of himself, as it were—his past, present, and future lives all at once—to become *maskil* (enlightened).

The Ari condensed the entire meditative procedure in the image of a man grasping one end of a bowed branch, shaking it vigorously, and thereby shaking the entire tree. A weak man would not be able to grab and shake the highest branch on the tree: "If he does not have the power . . . then the spirits inhabiting the attributes do not consider him at all, and they do not desire to bring themselves close to help him . . . for it is vain and of no use."

More explicitly than Rabbi Simeon, the Ari defines the "membranes" encasing each sphere. The outermost membrane, he says, consists of the light of the "Quarry of Souls"; beyond that is the light of the "Quarry of Angels"; and beyond that the "Darkening Light," or "Quarry of Husks" (matter). Further "membranes," or "halls" comprise the universe, the firmaments, the archetypal worlds, and the elements. Because each sphere consists of ten lights, which in turn themselves contain ten more, and those ten more, and so on, the universe contains levels without end. Only the proper man, uttering the proper *yichud* in a state of perfect concentration, may penetrate them all. Ezekiel's vision, according to the Ari, is called the "workings of the vehicle" because each sphere on the tree which he contemplated served as a "vehicle" for the next. Tearing through the veils of matter and human thought, he encountered the "Throne," which is actually another way of referring to the highest spiritual experience that takes place in the Quarry of Souls—the root of the patriarchs, whose souls are the very stuff of God's Glory. Only by yoking his mind, body, and soul to the Name (as the patriarchs had done) could the Kabbalist hope to emulate Ezekiel and transmit the divine light to himself and to the world.

Once a man had seated himself, visualized the tree and its spheres, and pronounced the *yichud* formulas, he could not stop, for not only was his own soul at stake but the "binding" of entire worlds to God as well. If he performed the exercise in a prone position over the grave of a favorite saint, he had to keep in mind that the great soul too was prostrating itself in the grave for the duration of the procedure. Or he could sit in his room and visualize a great white curtain emblazoned with a white form composed of the letters of God's Name, each "as tall as a mountain." Then he mentally interwove the letters, permutating them until they lost their apparent meaning and just as suddenly lined themselves up into words providing "answers" to his most profound spiritual questions. "But," the Ari warned him, "you must be careful of how you permutate so as not to bring chaos and disorder on your mind." Truly good advice to one who would assail the maze of lights, spheres, halls, guardians, and sacred names that Kabbalists call "contemplation."

PARALLELS TO TAOIST MEDITATION

I had almost despaired of separating the metaphor from the method, when I came across a clearly detailed description of a Chinese Taoist text on meditation which—except for the terminology—could have been lifted from the *Zohar*.

> The Taoist first transcends worldly affairs, then material things, and finally even his own existence. Through this step-by-step nonattachment he achieves enlightenment and is able to see all things as One.[2]

To this end, the Chinese mystic, like Rabbi Eleazar, also advocates practicing certain breathing techniques. What Eleazar

[2] Chang Chung-yuan, *Creativity and Taoism*, pp. 131, 157, 159.

refers to as the "four directions" of the breath, Tao-an, a fourth-century Buddhist master, calls "*Anapana,*" which he too divides into *four* techniques "which make use of the functions of the body." Taoist meditative practice also compares the human body to the macrocosm, focusing on the spine as the source of divine energy, which can be evoked by a combination of visualization and breathing. Like the Kabbalist, who "stirs the world above" by sitting down to his meditation here below, the Taoist reflects the outer world through the harmonizing of mind, breath, and body.

The Kabbalist's cosmic man and tree of spheres, as well as his corresponding "elements," have their counterparts in the Taoist's

> four seasons, five elements, nine divisions, three hundred and sixty days. Similarly, man has four limbs, five internal organs, nine orifices and three hundred and sixty joints. Heaven has wind, rain, cold, heat; man, similarly, has joy, anger, taking, giving . . . Man forms a trinity with Heaven and Earth, and his mind is the master . . .

Each organ of the Taoist's body is likewise analogous to an element, a direction in space, a season. And, as in the world of the *Zohar,* all are interdependent. The multiple symbols in Taoism, however, very specifically refer to meditative breathing techniques. "One grand heavenly circulation"—compare one complete "ascent" and "reversal" in the Lurianic *yichud*—moves the breath upward along the spine to the top of the head and downward through the face, encompassing the entire body as it returns to its foundation at the base of the spine. The Taoist exercise also begins as a visualization and ends with an actual physical sensation of "the circulation of the 'breath' as a heat current." Compare this with the Kabbalist's "light."

Various centers in the body are referred to by the Taoist by metaphorical names like "purple court" and "mystic chamber" —almost overlapping with the Kabbalist's "halls of the palace." Esoteric Taoist texts advocate "seeing" the breath move in conjunction with the conscious idea of controlling and directing it to various body centers. Like Rabbi Simeon, the Taoist meditator chooses to begin with contemplation of the highest, unmanifest point. He, too, is shaken by the ecstatic rush of light that ensues: "Sometimes one suddenly experiences a flash of light, which illumines the entire body beyond one's control."

"Unifying" the two centers at the heart and kidney is called "causing the Blue Dragon from the Court of Fire to descend and meet the White Tiger from the abyss of Water"—exactly as the Kabbalist would unite the spheres of *Beauty* (blue, identified with the sun and fire) and *Foundation* (watery, moon). When taken out of its mysterious wrappings and stripped of its religious overtones, the Kabbalist's tree of spheres, like the Taoist's heavenly and earthly "bodies," is clearly a breathing and concentration chart.

Professor Chang characterizes concentration on a specific point in the body as a stimulus to "the nervous system in that region." The spinal column, a veritable tree of nerve fibers and electrical charges, is subject to psychic stimulus as well as to physical shocks. According to him:

> When the practitioner constantly sends the genuine idea to the nervous system, it moves on unceasingly; a tremendous change in the electrical charges is effected and the current flow is greatly increased. As the operation in the serious practitioner goes on month after month, and year after year, the emergence of "lightning and thunder" within his nervous system will be the natural outcome . . . Here symbolic language is used to describe a physical phenomenon.

The same experience of being literally "illuminated" or bathed in light is described by fourteenth-century Taoists *and* thirteenth-century Kabbalists. Modern neurologists characterize the experience more blandly as "depolarization of the electric charges in the network of the nervous system." Spiritual or physical, the phenomenon relates to a very deliberate attempt on the part of the meditator to transform himself through intense concentration on various sensitive parts of his body in conjunction with systematic breathing patterns.

More remarkable still is the similarity between the Kabbalist's cosmic tree and the Taoist's "diagram of the ultimateless." Both are depicted as a series of ascending circles that lead to *Hsu* (non-being, Chinese) or *Ayin* (no-*thing*, Hebrew). The first circle, or gate, is the "Gate of Dark Femininity" to the Taoist, and the female *Sovereignty,* our world, to the Kabbalist. Both stand for the energy at the lowest center of the body that must travel upward through the breath, and merge with its "Lord," at the center of the brain, in spiritual union.

The second circle, referring to *Foundation* in Hebrew, is *Ching* (Essence) in Chinese—the place where "the breath is compounded." The following five spheres, four branching out to right, four to left, and one to center, represent the five elements, the "five movers" of the "lesser circulation" which, starting at the heart center, ultimately merge with the "grand circulation" of the breath. Like the Kabbalist's tree, these also are divided into male (right) and female (left), which eventually unite in the uppermost world of non-being—the spheres of *Wisdom, Understanding,* and *Crown* in Hebrew and the fused black and white circles *K'an* and *Li* in Chinese; over these there presides the empty white circle of *Hsu* (non-being, Chinese) or *Ayin* (no-*thing,* Hebrew).

Like the Taoist's "diagram of the ultimateless," the Kabbalist's tree is as close as his own spine; the "spheres," or nerve centers, are activated by his imagination; the "divine light" is drawn down by the engine of his breath.

4
The Path of Letters

For Jewish mystics, the Hebrew language has always corresponded physically to the things it designated. Merely writing a Hebrew letter could produce a unifying effect on mind and body, putting one in touch with the "higher" world. Imitating God, so to speak, the Kabbalist "created" himself anew by calling into being his deepest spiritual potential through manipulating letters—the ground, form, and sound of the physical universe, the tools with which God had created the world. Three primordial letters, the *aleph* (א), *mem* (מ), and *shin* (ש), contained all potential elements; twelve "simple" letters followed, serving as a channel for the divine energy which sustains the universe. Insofar as he is himself composed of elements, man, the microcosm, is "imprinted" by all of these letters on his own person. Meditation performed by a pure human being on any letter—as projected through its corresponding sphere, or divine attribute—was tantamount to meditation on the entire Creation. Comprised of the same basic substance as the stars, a man could become one with the furthest star; vibrating with the same energy as the birds, a man could learn the language of the birds. Jewish mystical practice literally assumes that the part may indeed be taken for the whole.

By taking the word inside out of itself, playfully shaking it loose from its denotative meaning, and melting it down as he led his rapt disciples from rational discourse to the realm of pure, non-verbal perception, the Kabbalah master (like the Zen master presenting his *koan* paradox) directed the novice out of the circular and constricting round of thought. Using thought and sound in stages, he moved beyond thought and sound: "Open your mouth in uttering the *aleph* [Hebrew A], and you extend your mind from the localized toward the boundless," said Rabbi Nehuniah ben Hakana. "For human thought has no end; through it, man may descend to the end of the world."

The Word intervenes between the ineffable and knowable God. As the tools for human speech, the letters combine to produce thought; as the implements of nature, they produce the elements, planets, sexes, and all physical beings. Engraved in the sphere of *Wisdom* on the cosmic tree, the Hebrew letters are the energy behind all descending manifestations of form, sound, and shape. For the Kabbalist who seeks to unite the letters to their original source in *Crown*, they present a composite name for, and experience of, the Absolute which called them into being. The letters cannot exist without the form provided them by the spheres which contain them. But the spheres themselves are, in a sense, illusory, mere images created by the limited human mind in its laborious ascent to the One.

Sounding very much like a Hindu Vedantist, Moses Cordovero put it this way:

> The Creator is Himself, at one and the same time, knowledge, the knower, and the known . . . There exists nothing which is not united to Him and which He does not find in His own essence. He is the type of all being, and all things exist in Him under their most pure and most perfect form.

Cordovero believed that man could imitate God by pronouncing the "divine language" with the intention of evoking its "essential nature." The sound of the Kabbalist's utterance ascends to the source from which all thought is born, unites

with the spirit residing there, and is transformed into a
"bodiless spiritual being" that uplifts man.

This kabbalistic view of language is charmingly interpreted
in a Tunisian version of a story from *The Thousand and One
Nights*. A Brahman named Padmanaba, trained in Kabbalah,
explains to his disciple how the letters of the Hebrew alphabet, when pronounced with the proper spiritual intention,
evoke their corresponding angels:

> "Each letter is ruled by an angel [which] is a ray of an outflow
> of the virtues of the Almightiness and qualities of God. The
> angels which dwell in the earthly and in the heavenly world
> rule those who abide in our earthly one. The letters form the
> words, then the words the prayers, and it is the angels who,
> designated by the letters and assembled in the written and
> spoken words, work the wonders at which ordinary men are
> amazed."[1]

To the Kabbalist the letters represent a combination of
name and form that comprises our physically known universe.
Like the physicist who is now attempting, through "quarks,"
to locate the simplest particle, the essence or fundamental
quality of matter, the Kabbalist, by turning "name" and
"form" (conveniently packaged in the pictographic letters of
the Hebrew alphabet, which includes "number" and "dimension" as well) into a kind of divine atom, pierces through the
letter to its essence, making every possible combination and
permutation of it afforded by nature, so as to leap beyond nature. To this end, he manipulates the first Name of God, that
quintessential force informing all matter. With a mighty
effort, he unites his own human energy with that which
radiates throughout the *Crown* of all that is, was, and will be.
Through the power innately occupying the word, he confronts
the permanent in the impermanent, the One in the many. A
letter, perceived thus, *is* what it represents: it is physical by
virtue of its being uttered by physical organs; it is spiritual in

[1] Quoted in Siegmund Hurwitz, "Psychological Aspects in Early Hasidic
Literature," *Timeless Documents of the Soul*, p. 194.

that it is linked to the world of angels; it multiplies to form the world of names and objects, but when reduced to its original sound, it becomes nothing more than the hum of the universe, vibrating in a place where light and sound merge in radiant silence.

The meditative technique known as *tzeruf*, permutation of letters, uses language to cut through its own structure and enables the mystic to reach the suprarational realm very quickly. The Kabbalist who practiced this extraordinary form of contemplation, studied a biblical phrase until it lost its rational meaning and, in the disorientation following repeated pronunciation of the now meaningless phrase, there suddenly thundered forth a "meaning beyond meaning." Combined with special breathing techniques and contemplation of body centers, meditation on the letters produced ecstasy almost immediately.

Impelled by their anti-rational bias, the thirteenth-century practitioners of *tzeruf* attacked their more cautious contemporaries along with Talmudists and the Jewish establishment in general. Abraham Abulafia, leader of this Spanish school which flourished alongside the *Zohar*, announced—among other things—that he had come to rescue the sleeping materialists from their "vainglory of learning."[2] Few followed his radical path directly, but many Kabbalists were influenced by the explicit technical manuals of instruction on permutating the sacred Name of God which Abulafia left behind. His mysticism rests on direct experience of the Divine and excludes everything else. Abulafia's own calling came to him in the form of a heavenly voice, crying, "Abraham, Abraham!" He replied, "Here am I," and the voice immediately launched into a detailed course in letter permutation—secret instructions which Abulafia later openly taught to Jew, Moslem, and Christian

[2] Material on Abulafia has been gathered by the author from manuscripts in the original Hebrew located in the following libraries: Jewish Theological Seminary Library, New York; Bibliothèque Nationale, Paris; Bodleian Library, Oxford; Hebrew University Libraries, Jerusalem.

alike. By closing himself to mundane experience Abulafia felt he would automatically open his soul to no other influence but God's. In his attempt to dislodge the mind from its worldly preoccupations, he juggled the Hebrew alphabet, contemplated the Name of God, and combined abstract and concrete language in an intellectually meaningless but mystically logical fashion to produce what he called "prophetic consciousness."

Of all Jewish mystics, Abraham Abulafia most nearly resembles the antic Zen master. Footloose, leaving all halakhic tradition behind him, willingly disclosing age-old "secret teachings" to the world, he sought in pure, non-cognitive thought, to capture the music of the spheres. In this pursuit, all languages became for him one language. His technique separated and reunited phrases and letters, divested words of their ordinary meaning, indeed, spun them out of recognition until their informing spirit electrified the body and mind. His method took the disciple in stages through *mivta* (articulation of the letters), to *mikhtav* (writing them), and, finally, to *mashav*, (contemplating them). Moving from gross material visualizations to finer spiritual ones, the Abulafian mystic eventually reached a state of ecstasy in which he was actually confronting the premanifest "spirit" behind each formed letter. *Dillug*, or skipping, consisted of observing the mind as it free-associated from one idea to another according to a set of flexible code words. Here, instead of forcing away distracting thoughts and images, the Kabbalist followed them by constructing them into sentences, breaking down those sentences into words, the words into letters, and the letters into light.

Combining and permutating the letters at night in seclusion, Abulafia's disciples experienced the same fiery sensations recorded by the *Merkabah* mystics twelve centuries earlier. Far from chaotic frenzy, his "irrational" system was carefully constructed. Assigning each letter to a corresponding body part, Abulafia warned his students to be careful not to cripple themseves by "moving a consonant or vowel from its proper position." Breathing and body posture also corresponded to appropriate vowel and consonant sounds. Personifications of the letters, angels like Metatron or Shaddai, made frequent appearances to mystics of the Abulafian school. At the point, however, where no visions at all appeared, the "exalted man" became one with his Creator. Masters of the Name, as these were called, were "no different" from God when they entered these states—sacrilege to the ears of a Jewish establishment steeped in logic, order, and dualism, which was soon to strike back at the "wild and dangerous" assertions of this pseudo-Messiah.

Direct confrontation with the *En Sof*, the Infinite, was more important to Abulafia than any visionary experience. That is perhaps why he played down the importance of the spheres as divine attributes. For him, the overriding significance of their cosmic power lay only in the mystic's direct experience of that power. Once he had felt and absorbed the light of the spheres, Abulafia's disciple had to learn how to permute the still more abstract spirit of the twenty-two Hebrew letters inhabiting them.

Though on friendly terms with contemporary Moslem mystics, the Sufis, Abulafia rejected their ego-obliterating trances in favor of contemplating the natural world represented by letters. Like all Jewish mystics, he preferred starting from the outside and moving gradually in. Therefore, he instructed his students to ponder deep theological questions raised in the scripture until their minds could no longer reflect on anything more than the very letters comprising the problem. Although the student initially attributed the solutions resulting from his concentration to rational intellectual processes, Abulafia proved to him that it was really the force of the letters "which influenced him through their motion and which concentrated his thought on difficult themes, although he [was] not aware of this."

Student accounts describe Abulafia as an easygoing, supportive teacher who led them cautiously to the highest practice of permutating the divine Names. With the *Sefer Yetzirah* (a first-century manual on letter contemplation) as his text, Abulafia allowed the disciple a two-week period for memorizing a letter and its correspondences. He later instructed the student to efface everything he had memorized, for even the highest spiritual forms would have to be transcended in favor of the formless Absolute. The less intelligible the divine Name, the higher its order. The less reason and intellectual control at play, the greater the spiritual force. Literal study of Torah, for Abulafia, served only to sharpen the intellect; the real "work" took place only in mystic trance.

"If today we had a prophet who showed us a mechanism for sharpening the natural reason and for discovering there subtle forms by which to divest ourselves of corporeality," he said, "we should not need all these natural sciences in addition to our Kabbalah." Abulafia's ideal prophet would of course reveal the combination of consonants and vowels which produce immediate ecstasy—as he himself was doing.

Despite his rebellious pronouncements, he adhered to the old Jewish concept of *madregot,* or levels. Even Abulafia's students could not rush, Sufilike, into immediate oneness with God, at least not before they had submitted to the typical process of mental, physical, and spiritual purification demanded by all Jewish mystical schools. Abulafia did differ from the others by forbidding intellectual work before engaging in contemplation, for even the highest form of intellectual Torah study, he argued, was a coarse obstruction to the clear light of the spirit. In addition to the usual prescription for solitude, he added a pleasant touch to the proceedings by decorating the meditation area with sweet-smelling greens. But he did not differ from even the strictest German pietist in ordering his disciples to immerse in the ritual bath, to fast, and to abstain from sexual intercourse before sitting in meditation.

The real discrepancy between Abulafia and other Jewish mystics, like his contemporaries the German Hasidim, lay in his willingness to reveal the practices which they hid so assiduously from the uninitiated. Abulafia broke all the rules of the Jewish mystical brotherhood when he disclosed to the world its sacred techniques for contemplation of God's Name.

ABRAHAM ABULAFIA: MASTER OF "TZERUF" (LETTER PERMUTATION)

Abraham ben Samuel Abulafia was born in Saragossa, Spain in 1240. His father, who guided him in his study of the Bible and Commentaries, died when the boy was eighteen, and the family moved to Toledo. Two years after his father's death Abraham journeyed to the Holy Land in search of remnants of the ten lost tribes who were rumored to be living near the mythical river Sambatyon. He never got beyond Akko (Acre), on the coast of Palestine, however, the Moslem-Christian wars interfering with his expedition. From Akko he traveled to Greece, where he found a wife with whom he settled down for the next ten years. Then, prodded by an unfulfilled yearning for initiation into Kabbalah at the hands of a true master, Abulafia set out once again—this time for Capua, Italy, where he made a careful study of Maimonides' *Guide for the Perplexed* under the tutelage of Hillel ben Samuel of Verona, a physician and scholar.

Soon after returning to Spain Abulafia gathered his own students around him; but the first group, as he discloses in his autobiography, "went astray." Enemies accused him of teaching trinitarian doctrines that were turning young Jewish scholars to Christianity. Abulafia countered the attacks by saying that these students had been dabbling in magic from the outset.

At the age of thirty-one, while residing in Barcelona, he received the famous prophetic "call." Although confused about the exact nature of his mission, wandering still in search of the ideal master, he didn't hesitate to write books about his prophetic inspiration. At this point, too, he picked up and made an in-depth study of a commentary on the *Sefer Yetzirah*. The author of the commentary on this arcane and extremely influential handbook for mystics was one Baruch Togarmi, the man who was soon to become Abulafia's long-sought-after teacher.

The year 1273 found Abulafia at the center of a sizable kabbalistic circle, actively teaching, writing, and outlining his particular system of *tzeruf*. Using a pseudonym corresponding in numerical value to his own name, Abulafia circulated his meditation manuals under titles like *Splitting of Names*, and presented a mystical commentary of his own on Maimonides' *Guide*. Influenced by the intricate kabbalistic style of his mentor, Togarmi, Abulafia freely sprinkled his texts with codes, acrostics, and number-letter puns to simultaneously befuddle his persecutors and communicate freely with knowledgeable Spanish mystics like Joseph Gikatilia, a respected member of his circle. Always compelled to justify his career in the eyes of the Jewish (and Gentile) authorities, Abulafia kept valuable records of both his own and his followers' activities. His spiritual autobiography, *Otzer Eden Ganuz*, (Hidden Treasure Garden), depicts a man with a missionary purpose who traveled frequently between Greece, Italy, and Spain. In several manuscripts, also characterized by the typically Abulafian rhetorical, personal, and exuberant style, he portrayed himself as a self-made visionary and chastised certain disciples for straying from the one true (Abulafian) path.

THE MYSTICAL RABBLE ROUSER

In 1280, prey to a sudden vision urging him personally to condemn the notoriously anti-Semitic Pope Nicholas III, Abulafia made for Rome. Here at last the religious Jewish establishment saw its opportunity to be rid of the mystical rabble rouser. In joint accusation with the Christian authorities, the Roman rabbis tossed his fate to the Pope—who instantly ordered him burned at the stake. Before he had even entered Rome, Abulafia was sentenced to imprisonment and death, the firewood duly prepared for his arrival in the city the next morning. It was the eve of Rosh Hashannah, the beginning of the Jewish New Year and the High Holy Days. Abulafia sat a few miles from the city, meditating all night. When he appeared in Rome the following day, he was informed that the Pope had died during the night. Convinced that it was a miracle of his own making, Abulafia entered the Franciscan prison that had been prepared for him—and was released only twenty-eight days later!

The Pope had lost the fight, but the Roman rabbis were determined to persist. Their continued persecution of Abulafia after his liberation from prison drove him to Messina, Sicily, where he remained with his loyal disciples and wrote major kabbalistic treatises, such as *Or Ha-Sechel* (Light of the Intellect), *Sefer Ha-Tzeruf* (Book of Permutations), *Mafteach Ha-Hokhmoth* (Keys to Wisdom), *Sefer Ha-Cheshek* (Book of Enthusiasm), and *Chayey Olam Habah* (Life of the Future World). But Abulafia was congenitally disposed to making provocative public statements; ten years after his release from prison in Rome he was announcing the Jewish Messianic Year to the world. Many Jews took the date (1290) seriously and, packing their belongings, emigrated to the Holy Land. Abulafia's rabbinical opponents, however, were also spurred into action. Rabbi Solomon ben Adret of Barcelona issued a document labeling Abulafia a dangerous charlatan. This time the unhappy prophet escaped to Malta, where he promulgated a series of treatises defending both himself and his meditative system. Most prominent among these is *Ve-Zot Le-Yehudah,* (And This, to Judah), an *apologia pro vita sua* ostensibly addressed to a disciple named Judah, but really intended as an open reply to Rabbi Solomon ben Adret. In this long philosophical poem on prophecy, Abulafia claimed that he was one of the few daring men born of all nations who had found "the steps of the ladder" leading to God. As one of the bolder prophets among them, he had "entered the palace of the Temple."

Abulafia went on to accuse ordinary Jewish spiritual leaders of encouraging ignorance about spiritual life and practice, contrasting them with worthy "Turks" and "Ethiopians" who permutated letters as an inducement to ecstatic vision. He chided the rabbis further for not learning the secrets of reincarnation or teaching their students about the divine powers residing in the human body. According to Abulafia, the rabbis had purposely ignored the knowledge beyond the five senses, limiting themselves to the safety of "tradition" and "hearsay" rather than embarking on the path to experiential "understanding." Tradition, he said, was nothing without the vehicle of the human body. Kabbalah, as old and as valid a Jewish tradition as any other, boldly made use of the human apparatus. Only change, new life, and new interpretations of the time-worn systems would revive them. Human beings, vehicles for change resulting from their spiritual experience, could vitalize the old traditions and make them worthy of being passed down to new generations.

Abulafia also accused the rabbis of burying themselves in philosophical Torah speculation and talmudic legalism. He contrasted these unfinished mental products with their noble contemporaries the Kabbalists who, on the one hand, contemplated the sacred Name through the medium of the tree of spheres (the Zoharic school) and, on the other (like himself), permutated the twenty-two Hebrew letters to gain prophetic wisdom. Neither practice, he concluded, was popular throughout the Jewish world; in fact, he remarked, these forms of contemplation were even unknown to most ancient Jewish sages. But this did not invalidate his claim that direct experience of *devekuth* (cleaving to God) rather than blind belief in esoteric scripture was the only truly "rational" way to approach God.

Citing his penetration of the mysterious *Sefer Yetzirah* as justification for his prophetic claims, Abulafia confidently stated: "I derived Kabbalah from [Baruch Togarmi's] twelve Commentaries [on the *Sefer Yetzirah*]." Despite his belief that the meditation on the cosmic tree was earlier in origin, Abulafia concluded against it: "But I have found the second [*tzeruf* method] to be more effective for implementation for those on the path to enlightenment." Prophets, he argued, received divine information from within their own minds and were thus passively limited to receiving varying degrees of higher light. Where biblical prophets had depended on grace, the Kabbalist *consciously* rose through meditation from light to light, clearly and deliberately impelling his thought through the primordial medium of the word. Ascending this mental ladder, he ultimately reached a point where human speech itself formed a "house" for God's Word. This man, said Abulafia, truly deserved to be called "enlightened."

In an apparent sideswipe at his competitors from the Zoharic school, Abulafia remarked that sphere contemplation was merely a "prelude" to meditation on the Names. He concluded the first section of his book with a self-congratulatory flourish: "I am the only Kabbalist to compile explicit books, according to [both] the sphere tradition and that of the Names. All my proofs and demonstrations are built on the mysteries of the Torah, both written and oral." He went on to exhort his disciple Judah—no less than his opponent Rabbi Solomon ben Adret—"Look into yourself and you will come to find the beginning of thought, and you will see that it travels through your body and limbs."

But the rabbinic establishment remained deaf to Abulafia's plea for legitimacy, and he died, disgraced in the eyes of all but a few loyal followers, soon after the "Messianic Year" had come and gone without incident. There is no doubt that, along with the Ari and the Baal Shem Tov, Abulafia is one of the great masters of Kabbalah. Beyond the Jewish world, his teachings influenced the Moslem Sufis and Christian mystics like his contemporary Pico della Mirandola. Every practicing Kabbalist from the thirteenth century onward, admittedly or not, made use of Abulafia's explicitly stated Hebrew letter permutations. Yet even today only Sephardic mystics will openly acknowledge it. Abulafia still remains a taboo subject in conversations among Jewish mystics. He openly defied the chain of secrecy established for centuries by masters who sought to hide the "tradition" from the world. Moreover, he brazenly claimed, in his *Light of Intellect,* not only to have single-handedly broken that chain, but to have made the esoteric knowledge accessible to ordinary men for the first time. His universalism made him popular among Christians and Moslems, for he taught what he felt was the right of every human being, Jewish or not, a foolproof exercise for marshaling concentration and avoiding distraction. Because he was personally grounded in the Jewish tradition, he fixed his attention on the Hebrew letters, sure in his belief that the human soul is literally bound to God's self-assigned Names. Convinced that Hebrew was a sacred language, he saw in each letter a key to human liberation. In this light, the priestly blessing that closes the last long daily prayer became for him a code of divine Names which the Kabbalist could use in much the same way the ancient Levites had in *their* services. His own firmly determined search for a teacher, resulting in his discovery of Togarmi, convinced Abulafia that a teacher was indispensable to the practice. And he dared to reveal the pronunciation of secret divine Names never explicitly mentioned in the Torah—combinations of letter, vowel, and consonant sounds that assisted the meditator in his leap toward undifferentiated consciousness, every man his own High Priest.

> The name of this path includes the mystery of the seventy languages, which is in . . . permutation of letters; it is the bringing back of letters to their first substance, or materialization, by utterance and thought according to the path of the ten spheres. No holy thing is ever less than ten.

There were, according to Abulafia, basically three ways for the Jewish mystic to obtain enlightenment in the past: sainthood, achieved by renunciation, like a *tzaddik;* devotion, or *hasiduth;* and prophecy. The way of Kabbalah offered in the *Sefer Yetzirah*, as interpreted by him of course, more quickly revealed the secrets of contemplation. More unique still was his *tzeruf* method of bringing letters back to their first cause.

The master of letters could not be given to fantasy, for it was too easy to succumb to morbid imaginings and insanity once a man had left rational consciousness. Abulafia therefore urged only those with keen minds who were without ambition and free of a desire for "miracles" to join him. He clearly outlined the stages of disorientation that overcame the "letter Kabbalist," preparing him for states during which he felt himself "climbing" a spherical, rotating ladder, while his thoughts, images, fantasies, and visions wheeled unceasingly through his head. This phase, called "locating Metatron with his revolving sword," denoted the mystic's controlled passage from the conscious waking state to the unconscious. Here, in the refining fire of the imagination, he tested and changed himself from an emotional, subjective individual into a detached and objective observer of his inmost thoughts and fantasies. The "higher" he went, the greater the barriers. Like the ancient *Merkabah* mystics, he too plunged into the enveloping cloud of gloom that hides the light; but Abulafia's disciple, more psychologically sophisticated, saw that gloom as a projection of his own "darkness," the ego's shield against the ego-shattering light of illumination. And he was willing, like the saintly Rabbi Simeon ben Azai, to die while gazing at the light.

Abulafia's *tzeruf,* or letter permutation system of Kabbalah, is divided into two major "gates," each of which is divided into paths, which are subsequently divided into parts. The first is called the "Gate of Heaven," the second the "Gate of Saints," or "Inner Gate." On entering each of these meditative states, Abulafia's disciple was instructed to visualize himself successively in the forms of the angels Uriel, Raphael, Gabriel, and so on. These once-terrifying "Keepers of the Gates" seen by *Merkabah* mystics, said Abulafia, were merely names for human tendencies which the meditator could subdue and conquer by personifying them as angels and letters. Since all human beings were imprinted by the divine letters with which God created them, the Kabbalist could restore his rightful divinity by reassembling himself, so to speak—that is, by turning his "letters" (tendencies) in a godly direction. Stimulating those dormant letters in protracted concentration, he can raise the divine energy in his body:

> After much movement and concentration on the letters the hair on your head will stand on end . . . your blood will begin to vibrate . . . and all your body will begin to tremble, and a shuddering will fall on all your limbs, and . . . you will feel an additional spirit within yourself . . . strengthening you, passing through your entire body . . . [like] fragrant oil, anointing you from head to foot.

Yet Abulafia did not stop there. Physical and emotional bliss might be indications of higher states of consciousness, but for mystics seeking more than visions, they represented only the first of the "fifty gates of understanding" located in the human body. A symbolic indication of the long way to go, the first "gatekeeper" was called *Az* (Thus).

The permutations of the Hebrew letters grew more "sacred" and more difficult as the Kabbalist progressed through the gates. In the earliest phases he practiced on simple nouns and pronouns, the alphabet, structure of words, parts of words, grafting one word onto another, creating "new" words. When he had become proficient at this, he was taught how to calculate the numerical values of the alphabet, first on individual letters and afterward on permutated letters, spelled-out letters, and names of numbers. Eventually he applied the technique of reversing the alphabet, the structure of letters, and phonic families.

When he had mastered the natural world of names, Abulafia's disciple moved on to the second gate, where he calculated the number value of the Names of God, reversed them, and ultimately, by meditating on the attributes inhering in those Names, approached pure perception and knowledge of God. Nonetheless, Abulafia assured his disciples that there were as many ways to approach the letters as there were human beings; "but you must do it on your own," he told them. He did suggest that they confine themselves to working with the five Hebrew vowel points, which corresponded not only to the five phonic families, but to the five fingers on each hand, to the five toes on each foot, and said that they were equally interdependent. Extending the analogy, he urged his students to remember that the vowels and letters were as interdependent as a man's body and soul.

No disciple was taken on before having passed certain tests in the "ways of God." Each had to possess specific kabbalistic *midot* (qualities), like devotion without ambition, patience, generosity, humility, and self-control, love of learning, the mental ability to absorb and memorize the techniques, and the capacity for detached self-evaluation. If he failed one of the tests, the disciple was given another chance. This time Abulafia presented the test more subtly, so that the novice was unaware of being under surveillance. If he returned willingly and revised the error, he was taken back. If he failed the second test, he was given three further chances. Having returned and been accepted under probation, he was not yet taught the actual meditation techniques until the master found him firm and ready. If he was headstrong and resisted the tests, the novice was sent away for good. Those "perfect, faithful disciples" who passed were inducted in a ceremony which included the master's promised protection for his charges and the presentation of ten permutations on the secondary Names of God—all clearly expounded. On these occasions Abulafia enjoined his new followers to see that even the medium of letters still restricted them to physical images. When they freed themselves of these, he said, losing all ideas about body, mind, and God, they would tear aside the masks covering spiritual truth. Images of angels appearing to a receptive man were really disembodied projections of that

man's innate prophetic power. All souls possessed the potential for unity with the Absolute; when this was universally recognized, it would usher in the Messianic Age.

During these sessions Abulafia informed his students that
all degrees of spirituality were subject to obstacles, which he
called *mastin* (witholders), personified by ancient mystics as
angels and even as Satan. His own aim was to train each disciple to prevent his particular witholders from dominating his
mind. Gazing into the "chariot," he said, meant gazing into
the letters of God's Name mentally constructed in the form of
a chariot. What the ancients described in their sensory disorientation was the vibrating colored light of the spheres that
manifested themselves after much intense concentration. Still
deeper states produced a merging of letters and spheres which
resulted in the famous "lightning flash" the *Merkabah* mystics
had called *chayot*. ("And the *chayot* ran and returned like a
vision of lightning," according to Ezekiel.) Even a mere
glance at the written Torah, said Abulafia, induced such
states when Kabbalists saw the letters as "white flame upon
black," reading scripture without separating phrases into logical order. Once he had surrendered the sense and punctuation
of the phrases, the Kabbalist would find that the entire Torah
literally merged into a combination of divine Names. For
these exercises he advised his students to read the ancient
manual of Rabbi Akiva; even Abulafia's contemporaries were
included on his syllabus, works like Eleazar of Worms' *Book of
Glory*, the anonymous *Book of Torah*, and the anonymous
Book of the Merkabah. But he warned his students, too,
against the many false meditation handbooks that proliferated
throughout the Middle Ages. These had to be avoided at all
costs, for their aim was worldly power and their method was
magic. Teaching his disciples to recognize such works when
they came across them, Abulafia derided certain magical instructions calling for "the left rib of a donkey that died a nat-

ural death" in combination with his own recommendation to burn incense and decorate the meditation area with herbs.

Let those who equate mysticism with inertia look into the *Sefer Yetzirah,* where images of "engraving," "inscribing," "hewing," "weighing," and "interchanging—drawn from the daily occupations of the mystics themselves—point to extremely difficult and sustained mental work requiring an alert brain and a healthy body. Abulafia reinterpreted the ancient images in the context of his own system. "Engraving" meant visualizing letters; "inscribing," meant writing them; "hewing" meant splitting them down to their essence; "weighing" meant permutating and calculating the number value of the letters, and "interchanging" meant substituting one letter for another. Human beings, he said, were not the natural masters of language but rather passive vehicles for it, the human tongue its physical transmitter. The practitioner of *tzeruf* therefore saw language as the external communication of messages between souls. As a mere physical convention, language, the "name" and "form" of things, was the Kabbalist's medium for changing nature. Such responsibility demanded great moral development, for in making contact with the informing spirit behind a word, a man transcended both nature and mind and connected immediately with divine energy. Without ever having heard of the commandments, a perfect man would automatically observe them—regardless of his conventional language—for he, like them, would be the physical embodiment of spiritual perfection. The 613 divine precepts that emerge from the Torah correspond to the number value of the letters in the title of the perfect man: *Moshe Rabenu,* Moses, our master. Likewise, the limbs and functions of the human body (248), together with the days in the year (365). Each limb is daily sustained by, and must function as, a commandment. As the Kabbalist "cleansed" his body and sharpened his mind by observing the commandments literally, physically, and spiritually, he opened himself to the higher perceptions inherent in them. He eventually so perfectly co-ordinated body, mind, flesh, and spirit with the letters of the Torah, that he *became* the Torah.

Abulafia's "short path" to enlightenment, with its prodigious amounts of memorized scripture, elaborate numerical and alphabetical codes and formulas, and rigid ethical requirements, seems no shorter than that of any other school of Kabbalah. And there was no hard and fast assurance of success once the disciple had embarked upon the path. But for this, too, the master had an explanation: the amount of "enlightenment" bestowed in each generation accorded only with what the times required.

ENTHUSIASM

Those who had turned their hearts toward enlightenment were always assisted according to their capacities by the spirit or divine attribute identified as "YHVH *Elohim Zevaot*" (a sign in His host). The disciple was instructed to recognize this "sign" in his enthusiasm (or lack of it) when he sat down to meditate. Another manifestation of this helping spirit was the disciple's easy passage into *devekuth* (cleaving). Starting with the typically Jewish preliminary contemplation of God's greatness, eternality, and availability to man, the Abulafian Kabbalist developed *cheshek* (enthusiasm). Repeated meditations of this sort so evoked the *cheshek* that a man became virtually impregnable to all thoughts other than the desire to see God. Permutations of the word *cheshek* yielded all the words for "desire." One of these, *kisupha* (yearning), represented the final "desire" which impelled the Kabbalist toward union. Reducing the words for "desire" down to the very essence or nature of "desire," his God-directed will had purified him of all worldly yearnings and, moreover, had transformed a negative trait into a positive one.

Abulafia depicted this process of "universalizing" limited individual thought as the meeting between the spheres of *Wisdom* (masculine) and *Understanding* (feminine) to produce the child called *Knowledge,* a hidden sphere on the cosmic tree. Having permutated the letters of the Torah (that vehicle for all name and form, dimension and extension, in space and time), the Abulafian Kabbalist transformed the mundane matter of human thought into a similar vehicle for spiritual enthusiasm. It was this "chariot" which would draw him closer to the Throne of Glory. "Enthusiasm" had given him material for the imagination and substance for the intellect. Through the medium of the letters, he mentally projected his desired goal. If his motivation was too weak, he could not project his will far enough. Like a man who wished to eat a piece of bread, he would have to project the quality or essence of bread into his imagination by means of the word (and letters) which formulated his desire for bread into a thought. Next, he imagined the market where he shopped for bread, the type of bread he desired, walking there, and so on—until the imagined experience of eating bread had been actualized by his going to the market to fetch it.

Turning from the outer world where the eye saw the letters, the Abulafian Kabbalist concentrated on the more personal world of the mouth that uttered them. Their sound vibrated in his ear and subsequently lodged in his yearning heart. If his heart was cold, he went to the master and received an exercise designed to stimulate yearning. Visualizing a pyramid of *alephim,* structured fifty-five to a side and ten at the center, he was told to concentrate on the letters comprising the number 120, the point of "completion." This, Abulafia told him, would condense all other desires into the one desire for *devekuth.* Combined with an intricate knowledge of his every thought, literally down to the letter, exercises like this one enabled the mystic to regard thoughts, without fear or hostility, as separate from himself. In this detached fashion he experienced them as if they were "talking to him from the mouth of another man." Visualizing the letters helped him understand what was being "said" to him; if he did not understand all of it, then he was still lacking self-knowledge. The perfect devo-

tee existed in the one Name of God, detached from all else
but it, purified from within and without before he had even
begun to contemplate its seventy-two sacred letters.

MEDITATION ON THE NAME

Once Abulafia had declared the disciple ready for meditation on the Name, he isolated him from everyone and everything associated with the everyday world. Excluding from his
mind all colors, objects, and images, the disciple poised every
muscle and even the slightest mental fluctuation on the business at hand—the great Name. When he was completely still,
he made the sign of the High Priest with his fingers and
chanted from the Psalms as he lifted his eyes toward heaven:
"Prepare my prayer as incense, the lifting of my palms like an
offering at evening."

Visualizing his head and body as a perfectly balanced scale,
his tongue its center, he drew a long breath and announced:
"*Beginning of the Beginning.*" Then, changing the quality and
tone of his voice, he "answered" himself by pronouncing one
letter of the Tetragrammaton (YHVH) with the vowel sound
aah. Allowing a brief interval, he spoke again in his own
voice, "*End of the Middle,*" responding in the "second man's"
voice with another letter of the Name, also accompanied by
the vowel *aah.* Lastly, he announced, "*Beginning of the End,*"
and replied with yet another letter. This segment of the chant
had produced one completed portion of the Name according
to the first of the five vowel sounds; the result would be "*Yaah
Haah Vaah.*"

The disciple lowered his hands (whose outstretched fingers
were symbolic of the cosmic tree with its five branches on
each side), placing the left one over his heart and the right
one immediately above it—a gesture representing both the
union of opposites and the physical and spiritual perfection of
the ancient High Priest who had evoked the Name before
him. The first chant evoked the image called "Throne of

Glory," located at the heart, from which there suddenly appeared a celestial guardian. The Kabbalist prostrated himself before the figure while permutating the second portion of the Tetragrammaton in reverse order, still using the vowel *aah*. Finally he rose and recited the third portion of the Tetragrammaton in the proper order. This tripartite pronunciation formed a tribute to "imagination," "intellect," and a combination of the two, respectively.

He began the next part of the exercise with the call, *"Beginning of the End,"* and replied with yet another letter of the YHVH, accompanied by the second vowel sound, *o*. Again he moved from the *"Beginning,"* to the *"End"* portion of the Name and corresponding part of his body, stopping at the heart, "seeing" the celestial projection, bowing before it while chanting in reverse order, and culminating with the third pronunciation in proper sequence. He placed the third formula through the same process, never forgetting the proper hand motions, head motions, appropriate vowel sounds, and breathings:

> One need only permutate the letters quickly back and forth in his mouth to evoke the "thoughts" of the heart which bring about higher perceptions . . . You will then understand the concept of "Upper" and "Lower" essences within yourself, and you will no longer need to bother yourself in seeking for books or friends or rabbis to teach you what you lack in wisdom; for your master is your heart, and your God is inside you. Ask Him everything and He will answer everything correctly.

Sometimes Abulafia gave his students a traditional formula for meditation on three verses in Exodus, each of which contained seventy-two letters that could be permutated to form the Name. Describing God's guidance of the Children of Israel in their forty-year desert wandering, the verses each begin with a reference to motion: "And he traveled . . . ," "He came . . . ," "He stretched . . ."—all expressing the movement of the cosmos from the center, to the center, and around the center (Exodus 14:19,20,21). When the Abulafian disciple permutated the first letters of each verse and accompanied the resulting pronunciations of God's Name with hand and head movements, he was emulating the identical motions with which God called the universe into being and which sustain it still. Concentrating on the "chariot," his body, he evoked the life force which, coursing through his spine, connected him to God. By probing the apparently random letters which comprise all of nature, he was guiding the "chariot" in a perfect display of spiritual "horsemanship," completely in control of all his senses. The word *"Merkabah,"* Abulafia noted, not only means "chariot," divine vehicle, but also "combining" and "grafting" of letters. It was this secret, kept hidden for so long after the disappearance of *Merkabah* mysticism, that he had come to teach.

The disciple only had to remember that the letters were merely emblematic of a premanifest state which was accessible to men in pure consciousness. Abulafia advised him to begin the practice of *tzeruf* with the accepting innocence of the child who absorbs the forms and sounds of the alphabet by memorizing them before learning to read: "See them as the strings of a violin which vibrate as the bow passes over them, and let them quicken your soul's innately divine music in the same way."

The most advanced form of letter contemplation—permutating the *Shem Hameforesh*, or Specific Name—was taught only to disciples who had passed all the earlier tests and forms of meditation, who abstained from wine, were older than forty, and entirely free of anger. When such a student presented himself, said Abulafia, the teacher was obliged to give him the knowledge, whether orally or in writing. This final phase included disclosing the deepest mysteries of sex and creation, knowledge of which demanded *perfect* recognition of scriptural passages and their permutations without the slightest error or distraction. Anything less spelled injury and even death. When the disciple was ready, Abulafia advised

him to sit in his secluded meditation chamber without revealing his activities to anyone:

> Take each letter of the Name and vocalize it with a long
> breath. Do not breathe between two letters, only hold the
> breath for as long as you can, and then rest for one breath. Do
> this with each and every letter. There must be two breaths
> with each letter, one to hold it in during the utterance which
> *moves* the letter, and one for rest in the interval between
> every letter . . . Each single breath is comprised of an inhala-
> tion and exhalation. Do not pronounce the word with the lips
> between the exhalation and inhalation, but allow the breath
> and vocalization to emerge while you are exhaling. Visualize
> the nostrils and mouth in the form of the *segol* [vowel point
> for the sound *eh:* ˙.˙] You must know the letters by heart to
> perform this exercise.

At the appointed hour, the Abulafian Kabbalist began permutating the letters of the Tetragrammaton (YHVH) with
each of the five vowel sounds until he had accomplished every
combination of the twelve possibilities given him by the
master. Rhythmically "moving" them mentally throughout the
centers of his body as he charted his breath and combining
them with other letters of the Hebrew alphabet, he began
with *yod*, the letter representing the primal point in the
premanifest world and the solid in the world of matter. The
heh, second and fourth letter, stood for the breath of the spirit
and a plane in the world of geometry; while the *vav* represented a line. His own head was fire, his belly water, and his
heart air—the elements corresponding to the Tetragrammatic
letters.

"SHEFA": THE DIVINE INFLUX

The best hour for *tzeruf* meditation was midnight when,
wrapped in prayer shawl and phylacteries, surrounded by
many brilliantly lit candles, the Kabbalist started writing the
sacred letters in black ink on white paper. Gathering speed as
he permutated them, he felt a warm, glowing sensation at the

heart, the sign of the descending *shefa,* or divine influx. Singing certain names according to prescribed melodies, he attained ecstasy with the same sensations of air, heat, rushing water or oil described by *Merkabah* mystics. "As your fathers have warned you," Abulafia reminded him, "beware of the fire that you not be burned, from the water that you not drown, and from the wind that it not harm you." For this was the moment when the soul so longed to escape the body that it could inadvertently result in the disciple's death. Abulafia therefore instructed him to ignore any trembling, tears, or even pleasant sensations that might occur, lest he be unprepared for the *shefa,* which rushed forth from his lips in a torrent of words and unintelligible phrases.

At this point the alert disciple imagined himself seated at the center of a circle of angels who helped him to unravel the celestial message: "The letters will arrange themselves into answers so quickly that the tablet and pen may fall from your hands." The expanding radiance of the divine influx threatened annihilation, but Abulafia's devotee continued nonetheless, sure in his knowledge that his spirit would survive the body's death. The weaker his link with his body, in fact, the stronger and more vital grew the soul. "This," said the master, "heralds the realization that you have achieved the level of higher consciousness."

Upon returning to normal, the Kabbalist covered his face and slowly emerged from trance. To ease the "descent" from that high place, he inhaled the fragrance of spices. Then he ate a light meal before returning to his life's routine. Abulafia called the entire procedure "choosing life." If, after all his effort, the *shefa* did not infuse him, the disciple was enjoined to permutate the Tetragrammaton according to a formula that would spell "King"—all the while moving his head up and down to the sound of the vowels *O* and *I,* forward and backward to the *U,* right and left to the *A* and *E*—which commemorated the presence of the "King" in the six spatial directions. If repeated permutation of this kind still didn't bring down the light, he was told to "cry and repent," for it was considered a certain sign of his unworthiness. But Abulafia was an encouraging master; even at the most apparently hopeless point, he provided his students with further contemplative techniques. The final assignment, permutation for the Name inherent in the word *avoa* (I will come) meant that the student had hit rock bottom. "Be careful not to blame God," the master chided him, "for the emptiness is in yourself."

Sometimes the letters sprang to life of their own accord, "speaking" to the mystic for as long and as profoundly as the duration and depth of his trance. To those who permutated them in the form of *Ofanim,* the winged angels, they "flew" forth from the page, transmitting the mystery at Sinai. The possibilities were endless. Combined names of the powers impelling nature enabled a man to change nature. Should he wish to dry up the flow of the sea, he merely visualized the word *yam* (sea) at his heart, the symbolic center of the world, adding to it the words *ya ba sha* (dry land). Combining the words, he concluded with *meyabesh* (to dry up) and correspondingly effected its reversal in nature! This, Abulafia stated, was how Moses dried up the Red Sea.

Irrespective of his purpose, the Abulafian Kabbalist always began his contemplation by focusing on the crown of the head, or *Beginning of the Beginning;* then moved down to the middle of the face, or *Middle of the Beginning;* and finished that segment by concentrating on the back of the head, or *End of the Beginning.* Similarly, the topmost point of the heart, the center of the heart, the back of the heart, and so on downward through the abdomen to the base of the spine.

LETTERS THE SIZE OF MOUNTAINS

A fascinating testimonial left by one of Abulafia's own students, Rabbi Shem Tov the Sephardi, points to the success of the *tzeruf* method. Shem Tov the Sephardi started as a philosophical skeptic who had examined other systems first. Under the Sufis, "who divest themselves of all sensory perception by repeating the name Allah over and over again . . . until they are ecstatic," he was initiated into the mystical life. Seeking a more intellectual approach, he left them and joined the school of Ben Sira, a thirteenth-century philosopher who had his students focus on a specific problem after they had relaxed their minds with a drink or two of wine. After a short period of concentration, the "answer" to the problem emerged through a series of images or words, assembling themselves in the form of letters.

Shem Tov the Sephardi's interest in Ben Sira's technique led him to Abulafia, whose interpretation of the *Sefer Yetzirah* he found most effective of all. When asked to permutate the letters of the alphabet until they made no sense, his old skepticism revived. But thinking he had nothing to lose, Shem Tov the Sephardi cleared his mind of extraneous thoughts, sat down with pen, paper, and ink, and started permutating the letters. At the first stage of deep concentration he was stunned to see a light emanating from his own body. But having been forewarned by Abulafia against deflecting his attention from the exercise, he persisted.

Within two weeks his concentration had grown so profound that he no longer possessed a sense of his body when he was permutating. Combining the seventy-two-lettered Name according to the passage in Exodus, Shem Tov the Sephardi found the letters expanding "to the size of mountains" in front of his eyes. At first he feared he was losing his reason; his body trembled, he was sweating profusely. But he regained his composure, sat up, and continued permutating the letters. Again they expanded to great size. Four or five times he tested the procedure to see if it was not indeed an hallucination. Finally convinced that he had not imagined the entire episode, he came to Abulafia, asking for an exercise which would enable him to tolerate and sustain the tremendous force that seemed to emanate from his heart as he permutated the letters. The master replied that the power had come from God; he was not to be afraid of it.

For two sleepless nights Shem Tov the Sephardi meditated on the Name. Concentrating every fiber of his being on the movement of the letters, he again lost all sense of body and time. During this second stage he was beset by tremendous pressure in his forehead; nevertheless, he continued—though at one point he was convinced that his head would burst from his superhuman efforts to maintain unbroken concentration. Emboldened, he permutated the awesome explicit Name, the *Shem Hameforesh*, as he had been taught—and was immediately gripped by fear of dying. Praying with all his might, Shem Tov the Sephardi bravely continued permutating the letters of the highest Name of God, whereupon he was overcome by spiritual rapture of such intensity that he felt himself soaked from head to foot by a sudden rush of warm oil.

"There is no proof of this discipline," Shem Tov the Sephardi confides to other aspiring practitioners of meditation on the Name. *Rid yourself of finite preoccupations, divest yourself of the selfish ego, surround yourself with greens in an isolated room, recite the Psalms*, he advises them. *Then move the letters about, and see what happens. Do not be afraid to take your mind to the extremes of what appears to be illogical thought. Write, then pronounce, the sounds; eventually they will slip out of your conscious control until the mind turns itself inside out, as it were, and becomes a clear mirror in which you see your true Self. If you are dogged by "witholders," then you must further purify your mind before sitting in meditation—or else, like Rabbi [Simeon] ben Zoma, you will become insane.*

ISAAC OF AKKO:
"KILL THE SELF FOR THE TORAH"

Another practitioner of the *tzeruf* school, a contemporary of Abulafia's and an important teacher and philosopher in his own right, was Isaac of Akko. A work entitled *Miryat Ey-nayim* (What the Eyes Can See), Isaac's kabbalistic explication of Nahmanides' early speculations, still serves as a handbook for Jewish mystics. His own diary of revelations, visions, and advice to disciples, *Otzer Ha-Chayim* (Treasure of Life), attempts to prove that permutation of Hebrew letters is the quickest and surest route to spiritual enlightenment. Parts of his diary, in fact, were written while he was in a state of trance resulting from the mental manipulation of letters. Like Abulafia, Isaac postulated three stages preceding illumination: renunciation, *hasiduth* (devotion), and prophecy. But he added to them his own uncompromising, monistic tone. Devotion was represented by the performance of spiritual acts which entailed permutating the Tetragrammaton only while concentrating on Nothingness. Detachment was raised to an ascetic level not found in Abulafia's system. And solitude, according to Isaac, meant total hermitic withdrawal from the world.

This ascetic disposition gave rise to an attitude called *histapkut* (making do). As Isaac put it: "What is good for the body is bad for the soul and vice versa . . . for the soul [seeks] to attach itself to the . . . peace supernal . . . and from this comes great discomfort to the body, in the form of mortification, and mental stricture in meditation . . . all necessary conditions for reception of the Holy Spirit." In short, Isaac of Akko told his students to "kill the self for the Torah." Echoing Abulafia, he chastised the "philosophical" rabbis who contented themselves with the notion of a hidden, transcendental, third-person version of God and encouraged his students to seek direct experiential knowledge of God through His Name. Although Isaac's meditative exercises were based largely on the same technical system revealed by Abulafia, Isaac initiated certain procedures of his own. Assuming that each of the ten spheres contains God's Names, he divided the visualizations into four worlds along the tree: the Void; the premanifest; the world of attributes, where forms were visible; and the lower world of physical permutation.

With the aim of shooting up to the highest world almost at once, Isaac advocated constant meditation and sensory deprivation. This regimen, he believed, would make the Kabbalist's mind so ethereal, so wearied of "created things," that he would even skip the death-fearing stage of the *shefa* and, like Rabbi Simeon ben Azai, gladly embrace the Void at once. Isaac praised those who, like Rabbi Akiva, could "run and return" from higher consciousness, but his heart was obviously with the martyrs of the spirit who never "returned."

His emphasis on sin and suffering makes of Isaac a less attractive teacher than the generous and impulsive Abulafia. But the two masters were equally fervent in their dedication to the sacred Name and were equally committed to seizing knowledge of the Absolute while incarnated in the human body. In his enthusiastic embrace of suffering, Isaac advised his disciples to remember Rabbi Akiva's martyrdom, as well as his return from the highest world in meditation. He encouraged them to repeat it symbolically in their own asceticism, but undoubtedly chose to play down the historical circumstances surrounding the event. Akiva did not actively seek martyrdom but was forced to accept it, dying heroically at the age of ninety.

More significant for Kabbalah practice than his dour instructions on martyrdom was Isaac's unique reinterpretation of the Mosaic experience and his practical adaptation of its symbolism. Legend claims that "Moses saw the Torah written in the air of the heavens in black fire on white fire." Isaac of Akko formed a mandala with the images of air, mountain, and fire, instructing the disciple to "climb" the mountain to the highest point in his concentration and "lift" his eyes, letting them rove across the sky (emptiness) until they focused on the horizon point where sky and earth met. Within a visualized circle in the sky, the Kabbalist next "inscribed" the entire Torah, from the first *B* of *Bereshith* (Creation) to the last *L* of "Israel," the final word. This was most likely performed according to a shorthand version denoted by letters representing each verse. He gazed intently at each tightly crammed letter, imagining it stamped on white parchment. In the hair's-breadth space between letters and beyond their imprint, he saw a "white fire" so radiant that it dimmed the sun. The letters themselves were deepest black. Soon the entire vision merged into a spinning blur of black on white, the circle of letters and flames no longer divided into any recognizable beginning, middle, or end.

The Kabbalist held the spinning vision in his gaze for as long as he could, watching the unintelligible permutations that led him to the *Crown* of pure light. In this form, said Isaac, the "wondrous circle" of Moses, later called the "apron of King Solomon," had descended through the ages to the masters of the Name.

LATER REFLECTIONS ON "TZERUF"

By the eighteenth century, however, even Isaac's methods (not to speak of Abulafia's more revolutionary school) had become obscure and frightening to lesser Kabbalists. Chayim Yosef David Uzieli, an admirer of *tzeruf*, came across a pamphlet of Isaac's describing the method in some detail. Shrinking from the daring formulas contained there, Uzieli hid the book, convinced that permutation of the Tetragrammaton was not for his age. "Although we might stumble inadvertently across some knowledge, we are in danger of confusing the divine order in our minds. We must know God's greatness, and partake in the mysteries of the Torah . . . without making use of the Name," he declared, echoing the opinions of his rationalist age.

Kabbalists were never again to enjoy the freedom of openly permutating the Name. As early as the sixteenth century they were already using elaborate metaphors like the following to hide the plain directions given in Abulafia's and Isaac's texts:

_ approach the white fire
 the works of the *Merkabah*
_ a short and long path
Beautiful and good
In the mystery of the *Pardes* which is known
        to those who meditate on concepts known to us
        through this wisdom,
And know how to bend their heads like a reed
        between the knees until they have nullified the senses,
And then, having no sensations, see the supernal Lights
Constantly, in actuality and not in metaphor.
And it is necessary for the Master to stand over him
        the first time he does this so that he may be
Trained to bring his senses to normal—
Only then is the man initiated to his heritage . . .
Not to peek and be stricken . . . when he comes to
        see the face of the Lord.[3]

The spheres on the tree were co-ordinated with the letters
and soul and body parts by the sixteenth-century mystics of
Safed.

CROWN=*Aleph* and unifying level of soul.

WISDOM=*Beth* and ascending and descending level of
    soul.

UNDERSTANDING=*Gimel* and undifferentiated conscious-
    ness.

LOVING-KINDNESS=*Daleth* and animal self at its highest
    point.

JUDGMENT=*Heh* and spiritual consciousness tied to the
    body by the nexus of breath.

BEAUTY=*Vav* and the blood.

ENDURANCE=*Zayin* and the bone.

MAJESTY=*Chet* and the flesh.

FOUNDATION=*Tet* and the sinews.

SOVEREIGNTY=*Yod* and the skin.

[3] Rabbi Joseph ben Abraham Ibn Tzayach, *Even Ha-Shoham.*

Kabbalistic Practices

According to Moses Cordovero, the names resulting from the combined letters are the exteriorizations of God's attributes which descend into human consciousness in the form of sound. By linking themselves to these higher sounds or vibrations, the prophets of ancient times came to see that all worlds, all stages of consciousness, all beings are resolved in the One. Competely egoless, these men taught the unification of consciousness through letters in the hope of leading all human beings to the liberated state they themselves had achieved. But, says Moses Cordovero, with the ensuing persecution and dispersion of the Jews, these generations of sages dwindled, and their methods were hardly put into practice any longer. "And the hearts diminished, and those who sought Torah found their strength growing too weak even to perceive simple things—and certainly not Kabbalah knowledge dealing with the details of the spheres."

Cordovero's own permutation manual, *Pardes Rimonim,* (The Pomegranate Orchard), is an extrapolation of Abulafia's treatise on vowel points. As filtered through Cordovero's lucid prose, however, the *tzeruf* method is more immediately accessible to laymen. All letters, he says, depend on, and emanate from, the Tetragrammaton (YHVH). This can be physically illustrated by the *aleph,* for example, which consists of two *yods* and *vav:*

אׂ

and totals twenty-six, like the Tetragrammaton itself. This is the physical idea behind combining the alphabet with its source through visualizing letters along with their vowel points and reducing them to pure sound. Meditating on words evokes the true, formless meaning of their hidden nature; moving the vowel points around them increases the Kabbalist's spiritual vocabulary. Standing alone, the Hebrew letters are soundless, inexpressible without the vowels. Vibrated by the human voice, the pronounced letter takes its place in the spatial-temporal world in which the Kabbalist measures the letter's length and accent. Since the letter *aleph* stands for the One, the unity, the Kabbalist pronounced it during the course of one breath, with an appropriate head movement determined by the shape of the accompanying vowel. For example, combining the *aleph* (*A*) with the *yod* (*Y*), first letter of the Tetragrammaton, and the vowel called *cholam* (*O*), he took a deep breath and exhaled, having mentally pronounced the sound of the letter *aleph*. He looked straight ahead toward the East with his head slightly raised, thereby emulating the vowel *cholam* which is represented by a straight line with a point at the upper left: ֹ

Each chant of the combined *aleph cholam* and *yod cholam* (*AO YO*) was uttered in a perfectly empty state of mind with raised head, breath held and released, and was completed when the Kabbalist moved his head upward to simulate the point at the top of the *cholam*. In this fashion he ran through the entire alphabet in combination with each letter of the divine Name, according to each of the five vowel sounds, head motions, and breaths. The Ari, for example, had allotted specific vowels to individual disciples, recommending that they meditate on the Tetragrammaton using only these. Mistakes in pronunciation, breathing, or head motions brought the Kabbalist back to the beginning of the series. When he grew apprehensive or was otherwise interrupted, he prostrated himself in prayer. If family affairs or professional duties were too distracting, he did not meditate. Modern Kabbalists do not practice *tzeruf* at all.

5

The Path of Ecstasy: Hasidism

Thanks to the efforts of philosophers like Martin Buber and
Abraham Heschel, the mysteries of the Hasidic experience
have been revealed to the twentieth-century reader. Popu-
larizing campaigns on the part of the ubiquitous Lubavitcher
sect, particularly on the streets of large American cities, have
also called attention to these Jewish mystics. Romantic tales
and legends of the Hasidim abound; even the Broadway stage
has shared in disseminating both real and imaginary information about them. Many people identify them with long
flowing earlocks, black caftans, white stockings, patent-leather
pumps, and large fur hats. Some Hasidim today do dress like
that; but so do their opponents, the Orthodox *Mitnaggedim*,
or halakhic legalists. Some identify them as rebels within Judaism; yet most contemporary Hasidim are as rigidly Orthodox, as punctilious about their ritual life, as the most unenlight-
ened fanatic living in the Mea Shearim quarter of Jerusalem.
Some identify them as ecstatics; Hasidim do tend to sway and
dance when they pray, but most Hasidic synagogues resemble
any other synagogue, except for a few little peremptory efforts
at dancing on the Sabbath. And if you are a woman, you can
hardly tell what is going on at all because you have been put
behind a screen which blocks out everything but the sound of
desultory foot shuffling that today passes for Hasidic "ecstasy." If you are lucky enough to cram yourself into the

Lubavitcher synagogue in Brooklyn on a festive holiday, you may catch a glimpse of the dancing Hasidim, but you will find that nowadays vodka, rather than inspired song, induces bliss.

More written information about Hasidism exists than about all other schools of Jewish mysticism combined. The movement enjoyed the privilege of having brilliant and prolific philosophers to pen its principles, colorful saints to spread its legends, and—by not extending further than Eastern Europe—a circumscribed geography. Hasidism took Jewish mysticism out of its Oriental wrappings and Westernized it for the first time. The secrets of the *Merkabah* lie buried with the sages; the *Zohar* is still too opaque for most men to penetrate; manipulation of the sacred Names is for the elect and the Lurianic Kabbalah for members of an esoteric community. Only Hasidism is mysticism for the masses. Nothing more than simple prayer comprises its method; one need only surrender to its luminous *tzaddikim* in order to set foot on its path. Like Buddhism, it was initiated by a reforming holy man, a visionary democrat who rebelled against the dry, crabbed, and pompous ritualism into which the Brahmans of his faith had fallen.

Israel ben Eleazar, the Baal Shem Tov, or Master of the Holy Name, took the cosmology and practice of the Lurianic Kabbalah and made it accessible to the capacities of ordinary men. The heart of his teaching is *devekuth*, cleaving to God, but a far more personal and emotional version of *devekuth* than we have encountered before. The Baal Shem Tov emphasized *devekuth* in the "here and now," not by means of fasts and self-mortification but through joyful celebration of the Divine in everyday life. For him "meditation" was man's delighted awareness of himself in the midst of living. Physical acts, intended as worship of God and performed in a state of "cleaving" to the Absolute, became religious acts. Alien or distracting thoughts were products of the husks of matter which had interspersed themselves among the divine lights; so the Baal Shem Tov advised his disciples to distill the holy sparks from even these seemingly "sinful" thoughts by examining them and, if necessary, "correcting" them or discarding them altogether.

Kavanna (concentration), too, was reinterpreted to suit the immediacy of Hasidic mysticism; no longer reserved for synagogue prayer and meditation in solitude, it was brought out into the market place. When a cart driver confessed to his master that he could not get to services on time and therefore feared that he was not serving God properly, the master asked him if he accepted poor travelers into his cart without payment.

"Yes," replied the Hasid.

"Well then, you are serving God as if you had been in the synagogue," the master assured him.

Kavanna, or concentrated awareness directed toward selflessness, became an active part of the Hasid's daily ritual performance.

Hitlahavut, the Hasidic brand of enthusiasm, seeded the way for the comic spirit that characterizes the movement and distinguishes it from all other schools of Jewish mysticism. Hasidic enthusiasm was part of joy, and joy was not otherworldly bliss but earthy humor. In many cases, the comic spirit of Hasidism approaches the "Crazy Wisdom" of the Buddhists. Among the Hasidim, antic masters abound, tweaking noses, embarrassing pompous rich men in public, and even arranging happy marriages for the children of their disciples. For the Baal Shem Tov and his followers, enthusiasm was the proof of one's contact with the divine reality. Ecstasy occurred not as a result of arduous contemplation of the worlds within worlds, but as a spontaneous outflow of energy in response to *this* world and to the God that lives in its every stone, crawling insect, and child.

Prayer, said the Bal Shem Tov, is only acceptable to God if it flows from a joyous heart. Enthusiasm, not suffering, was the "great way" for a man to unite with the upper spheres and "break through all skies in one act." The "small way" was the narrow fastidious observance of the commandments as performed by the legalists. The legends of the Hasidic masters therefore overflow with references to the wonders effected by prayerful holy men. Some were ecstatic in frozen silence; others swayed and chanted; still others turned somersaults on their way to the synagogue.

Miracles and wonders sat side by side with the earthy, even with the coarse and ugly, aspects of life in the *shtetl* (provincial Eastern European village) which, for the Jew, could mean instant annihilation at the hands of the anti-Semitic hordes surrounding him. Still, interspersed between its superstitions and amulets, demons and dybbuks, Hasidism provided broad cosmic perspectives for the wretched ghetto dweller, and endowed him with a sanctity that reached deeply beyond his ragged parochialism and penetrated his soul.

Psychologically, the Hasidim were the most sophisticated of all Jewish mystics. They democratized the Torah, wrested it from the hands of the privileged scholars, and brought it back to the ordinary Jew. According to the teachings of the Baal Shem Tov, only the individual himself can pierce the veil that hides God from man. Once a Hasid had achieved mystical *devekuth,* it was his obligation to "go public," as it were, to teach it to others. This gave rise to the sanctification of Hasidic masters, the worship of the *tzaddik* which, some feel, led to the downfall of the movement. Others see the *tzaddik* as the mainstay of Hasidism.

> The [*tzaddik*] strengthens his Hasid in the hours of doubting, but does not open his eyes to the truth. He only helps him to conquer and reconquer the truth for himself. He develops the Hasid's own ability to pray. He teaches him how to give the words of prayer the right direction and he joins his own prayer to that of his disciple, thereby increasing the power of the prayer and lending it wings.[1]

[1] Harry M. Rabinowicz, *The World of Hasidism,* p. 185.

The difference between other spiritual masters and the Hasidic *tzaddikim* is perfectly illustrated by the change in their title: *Rav* (Master), the respectful form of address, was transformed by Hasidim into *Rebbe*, a diminutive, personal, and untranslatable version of the word that denotes affection and, in later years of the movement, the disciple's complete surrender to his teacher.

As walking examples of the Torah incarnate, these *tzaddikim* not only preached (and never formally from the pulpit— but rather, as the Baal Shem Tov did, to groups in the market place or in the meadows) but loved their disciples and lived in constant contact with their spiritual and earthly needs. Their methods differed, but most *tzaddikim* used the medium of the story or parable as vehicles for their teachings. Some were saintly, others were gruff, all were sometimes clownish. There is, for example, a wonderful photograph of Rebbe Israel Alter, the old Rebbe of Gur, who died in 1948: a group of venerable, bearded Hasidim surround an ancient white-bearded *tzaddik* in long black caftan and enormous fur hat. The group is obviously out on a discursive stroll when caught by the photographer. Most Orthodox Jews refuse to have their pictures taken for they regard photographs as "graven images"; hence, in this photograph, one of the Hasidim shields his face with his hand. The Rebbe, however, is walking straight toward the camera, hunched over like a boxer with fists at the ready and, in perfect Jack Dempsey form, feigns to deliver the first blow—all with a perfectly beatific smile on his face.

THE BAAL SHEM TOV:
HUMAN, PRACTICAL, AND WISE

The Ari was ethereal; the Baal Shem Tov was practical. Once, after having advised that a sick person in a distant town be bled, he added: "I can see from afar, but send a messenger anyway." His supernormal powers were always accompanied by bits of homely wisdom. The followers of the Ari stressed their master's saintliness, but the Baal Shem Tov's disciples were most impressed by his humanness. His very own person became a channel for their *mohin degadlut* (expanded conciousness). Like the Ari, the Baal Shem Tov never wrote; all his teachings were orally transmitted until they were finally collected after his death in the notes of his closest disciples, Jacob Joseph of Polonye and Dov Baer, the Maggid (Preacher) of Mezerich.

Born around 1698 in Okup, in the western Ukraine region, Israel ben Eleazar was orphaned early and left to the care of the sympathetic Jews of his village. As with avatars in other traditions, the details of the Baal Shem Tov's life have been expanded to legendary proportions. Like the Ari's, the Baal Shem Tov's future greatness was also announced to his father by Elijah before the boy's birth. His soul was a supposed incarnation from a spark of Rabbi Simeon bar Yohai's.

An early prodigy, the Baal Shem Tov hid his wisdom under a mantle of laziness and near idiocy. He worked as a janitor in the local synagogue, but secretly studied Kabbalah all night. Then, much to the disapproval of his future brother-in-law, Gershon Kitover, the illustrious son of the late respected Rabbi of Brody, the Baal Shem Tov married the great rabbi's daughter. After attempting to dissuade his sister from her course, the scholarly Kitover condescended to give the young couple a wagon as a wedding gift and then sent them off. Israel and his loyal wife moved into an isolated retreat in the Carpathian Mountains, where he studied and meditated, and she collected lime which she sold for fuel to the inhabitants of the valley towns.

The years passed in this fashion until one day in May of 1734, the Baal Shem Tov descended from the mountains with his wife and announced to his brother-in-law that the time had come for him to reveal himself to the world. Convinced now of the Baal Shem Tov's holiness, the once-skeptical Gershon Kitover became his first follower. The Baal Shem Tov's fame as a holy man and healer spread quickly, and thousands of villagers flocked to him for spiritual encouragement, healing, comfort, and blessings. This popular phase of the Baal Shem Tov's activities was followed by one in which he trained disciples, thereby formalizing the mystical techniques for divine realization which came to be identified as "Hasidic." Brilliant disciples like the Maggid of Mezerich circulated the Baal Shem Tov's doctrines throughout the Jewish community, drawing many followers—and violent opponents as well. In 1760 the Baal Shem Tov died, but not before he had brought the Kabbalah down from the angels and placed it securely in the physical hands of men.

THE HASIDIC METHOD: PRAYER

Hasidism emphasizes one method of practice only: prayer. In its larger sense, "prayer" encompasses preparation, devotion, love and knowledge of the Torah, contemplation, *yichud,* *tzeruf,* and all the rest. In teaching his disciples how to pray, the Hasidic master taught them to meditate, though in a less conventional sense than, say, Abulafia or the Ari had done. Mystic states of consciousness were, for the Hasid, part and parcel of daily experience; therefore much of the practice alludes to maintaining a prayerful attitude in all circumstances. Only with the third generation of disciples, particularly in the intellectual writings of Shneur Zalman, the first Lubavitcher Rebbe, does Hasidism arrive at a philosophical crystallization of prayer as a "technique."

The saintly Rebbe Levi Isaac of Berdichev (1740–1809), famous as a compassionate defender of the Jewish people, indulged in fervent prayer that was most characteristic of the early Hasidim. He startled worshipers during one Yom Kippur service when he broke off the traditional liturgy, placed himself squarely before the altar, and demanded of God that He halt the persecution of Jews or else he, Levi Isaac, would remain fixed in that spot until God responded to his plea.

Another Hasidic master, Jacob Isaac of Przysucha, said: "When you are so engrossed that you do not feel a knife thrust through your body, then you are offering prayer aright."

Rebbe Uri ben Pinhas of Strelisk even went so far as to bid his family farewell every day lest he die of ecstasy during prayer without having said good-by.

Each in his own way was embodying the Baal Shem Tov's idea that man's prayer completes God, for man is a vital spark of the Divine:

> With every word and expression that leaves your lips, have in mind to bring about a unification [*yichud*]. Every single letter contains universes, souls and godliness, and as they ascend, one is bound to the other and they become unified. The letters then become unified and attached to form a word. They are then actually united with the Divine Essence, and in all these aspects, your soul is included with them.[2]

The Baal Shem Tov taught that to become one with prayer was to become one with God. Reaching such exalted levels of consciousness, the Hasid lost all sense of his physicality; no extraneous thoughts came to disturb him; no fear or constriction intruded on his joy. He was, as the Baal Shem Tov described it, "like a small child whose intellect has just begun to develop." Achieved through the words of prayer, the Hasid's *devekuth* was extended by love, for, like a lover, he held them fast and did not want to let them go. "Because of your attachment to each word," wrote the Baal Shem Tov in a letter to his brother-in-law, "you draw it out." Having thus removed the barrier between himself and the Divine, a man came to see that there had been no barrier there in the first place, no evil but the illusion of evil constructed by his own thoughts. In the Hasidic version, Ezekiel's vision of the souls who "ran and returned" was analogous to the human soul that wishes to run to its source but must nevertheless live in a body that eats, drinks, and earns a living and so *returns* to its earthly quarters.

[2] From Aryeh Kaplan, "Sparks in the Night."

When, however, the sense of self disappears with the annihilated ego, the soul soars aloft, unobstructed, like one of the angels. But even the idea of an upper world, said the Baal Shem Tov, was nothing more than another screen shielding the divine from man's vision. The Hasid, dissolving even the angelic hosts through concentrated prayer, reverted again to the state of No-*thing*ness. Like Abulafia's master of *tzeruf*, he too assumed the living nature of the Hebrew letters and sought to extract their essence. With devotion as his instrument, the Hasid could either speak extemporaneously to God or confine himself to the prescribed liturgy; in either case, he consciously manipulated the Word, that perfect condensation of divine energy which would restore him to his rightful place at the Throne. It did not matter how he dissolved himself in prayer, the important thing was getting to the high place.

Nevertheless, mystical exercises called "as rigorous as Yoga" by the contemporary British Hasidic scholar Louis Jacobs, were also part of the Baal Shem Tov's discipline. Combining memorization of the Lurianic *yichud* formula with the corresponding permutation of the Tetragrammaton, the Hasid might meditate, for example, while immersing himself in the *mikvah* (ritual bath). Upon entering, he assembled the letters of the word *mikvah*, the numerical equivalent of the phrase by which God identified Himself to Moses, (I Will Be) and meditated on their forms. Dipping his head under water, he contemplated the name *Agla* (Strengths), an acronym drawn from the initial letters of the phrase *Atah gibor leolam Adonai* (You are strong forever for the world, O Lord). In this fashion he immersed himself five times, combining and permutating the names of God derived from memorized phrases out of the Lurianic prayer book. So much for the so-called "spontaneity" and "illiteracy" of Hasidic prayer. The Baal Shem Tov's inner circle was in fact exceedingly educated in both *halakha* (legal tradition) and Kabbalah. His foremost disciple, the Maggid of Mezerich, disseminated his master's teachings, developing them according to his own sophisticated, philosophical style.

> Think of yourself as nothing and totally forget yourself as you pray. Only remember that you are praying for the Divine Presence. You may then enter the Universe of Thought, a state of consciousness which is beyond time. Everything in this realm is the same—life and death, land, and sea . . . but in order to enter this realm you must relinquish your ego and forget all your troubles.

> You cannot reach this level if you are still attached to physical, worldly things, for that means you are linked with the division between good and evil, the dualism included in the seven days of Creation. How then can you expect to approach the realm where absolute unity reigns?

> Further more, if you consider yourself as "something" and pray to Him for your needs, God cannot clothe Himself in you. God is infinite and cannot be held in any kind of vessel but one that has dissolved itself into No-thing.

> In prayer you must place all your strength in the words, going from letter to letter until you totally forget your body. Permutating the letters will bring you much delight, both physically, in your heart, and spiritually.[3]

AN ITINERANT PREACHER BECOMES
THE BAAL SHEM TOV'S DISCIPLE

Dov Baer (1710–72), the Maggid of Mezerich, had been a renowned talmudic scholar before entering the Baal Shem Tov's circle. His saintly disposition turned him away from the settled and respectable life of a scholarly rabbi and toward the humble lot of the itinerant preacher. His mystical turn of mind launched him on a path of such severe fasting and self-mortification that he became crippled and ill. So great was Dov Baer's agony that he sought out the healing of the Baal Shem Tov—ironically, an avowed opponent of asceticism.

[3] From "Collected Sayings," of the Maggid of Mezerich, tr. Aryeh Kaplan, in Kaplan's "Sparks in the Night."

When the lame preacher arrived in the Baal Shem Tov's distant village after an excruciatingly painful journey, the master invited him in and embarked on a frivolous discussion about his coachman's diet. Disgusted, Dov Baer returned to his inn and started repacking for his journey home. Suddenly there was a knock at the door and a messenger informed him that the Baal Shem Tov had something still further to say.

The Maggid reluctantly returned and was this time challenged to interpret a passage of Lurianic Kabbalah. This, thought Dov Baer, was more like what he had expected of the great master, and he launched into one of his typically brilliant discourses. When he had finished, the Baal Shem Tov said, "You have learned only the body and not the soul." Then, taking the book, he began discoursing himself. The Maggid suddenly felt the room grow warm and saw it filled with radiant light which only faded when the Baal Shem Tov stopped talking. Dov Baer thereafter became the Baal Shem Tov's chief disciple and public voice, expounding kabbalistic doctrine to vast numbers of Hasidim. When the Baal Shem Tov died in 1760, it was the Maggid who took the master's mantle. His own tenure was even more rigorous than that of the Baal Shem Tov's, however. His weak physical constitution further degenerating under the persistent attacks of the rationalist establishment led by the Gaon of Vilna, the Maggid died a broken, excommunicated "rebel." Only nine years later had the controversy settled enough for his disciples to publish his collected sayings.

An uncompromising non-dualist, the Maggid often employed images that curiously resemble those appearing in Eastern philosophical writings. Scholars compare him to Shankara, the eighth-century founder of the Advaita (Non-Dualist) School of Indian philosophy. Some of the Maggid's sayings could have easily appeared over Shankara's signature:

> Think of your soul as part of the Divine Presence as the raindrop in the sea . . .
> The [premanifest] world is not subject even to the com-

mandments . . . it is beyond even ethical action which, as action, is dualistic.

Before an egg can grow into a chicken, it must first totally cease to be an egg. Each thing must lose its original identity before it can be something else. Therefore, before a thing is transformed into something else, it must come to the level of No-*thing*ness . . .

THE HASID'S JOURNEY THROUGH THE UNCONSCIOUS

Through the medium of the Hebrew letters the Hasid transformed himself from a separate individual into the entire creation. Prayers, organized and written by illuminated masters, were the prescribed formulas with which he initiated the change. "Each physical thing," said the Baal Shem Tov, "as well as the Torah and prayers, also contains these twenty-two letters with which the world and everything in it was created." The righteous man standing at prayer could thereby lose himself in simple, formless Unity; the spontaneous words that might issue from his lips were themselves divine emanations, new formulas for those who would follow. For those on a lower level of spiritual achievement, the Baal Shem Tov advocated praying out of the traditional prayer book, for "looking at the letters will give you more strength to pray with feeling. But when you wish to yoke yourself to the higher world, it is best to worship with your eyes closed."

The *amidah*, or silent prayer portion of the daily service, was the place in which the Hasid found himself truly near to God. But even this "nearness" was qualified by the level he had reached in his meditation. Hasidic masters graded their disciples according to the four worlds on the cosmic tree outlined in the *Zohar* by Rabbi Simeon bar Yohai. Nearness in our material world of action represented the highest point in a mind still conscious of itself (the dualism of ordinary experience). Nearness in the world of spiritual beings was a higher achievement, but was still dominated by images. Only the individuality which had been totally dissolved in the Absolute could be said to have reached the highest peak in the highest world on the tree.

Employing the Ari's devices for mindfulness, the Baal Shem Tov's Hasidim, like their forebears, the Cubs of Safed, wrapped themselves in phylacteries as they prayed, the forehead box reminding them of the sphere of *Wisdom* on the tree and the center of wisdom in the brain; the arm straps recalled the sphere of *Judgment* which was intended to evoke the proper state of Awe. But the more earthy Hasid also saw in this ritual the symbolic tie between a man's head (spiritual aspirations) and the earth to which the straps bound him fast. "Prayer," said the Maggid, "is the ladder with its feet on earth and its head reaching to the heavens."

To eliminate distracting thoughts, the Maggid devised a system which divided all thought into seven modes corresponding to God's seven days of "building." In man, these seven days were equal to the seven lower spheres on the tree of life. On each level there were equally strong good and bad thoughts. The first stage in the Hasid's self-observation consisted of isolating the distracting thought and determining to which of the seven spheres it belonged: *Endurance, Foundation, Judgment,* and so on. "Bad" thoughts, said the Maggid, inevitably came from the negative spheres on the tree of death, the inverted counterpart of the cosmic tree of life:

> If the thought involves desire and lust, it has fallen from the Universe of Love; if it is a debilitating phobia, it is from the Universe of Fear . . . When you bind these thoughts to God through Love and Fear of the Creator, you can return them to their source . . . Each thought can [thus] be elevated to the [original sphere] from which it fell.

These convenient symbols facilitated the Hasid's journey through the unconscious. Without an honest self-analysis, during which he confronted and examined each thought, "good" or "bad," and carefully traced it to its origin, he could never hope to obliterate *all* thought.

Taking the hint from Abulafia, perhaps, the Maggid advised his disciples to break up each thought into its component letters and to meditate on each letter without allowing any rational or discursive mental activity to take place. By dissecting the thought letter by letter, the Hasid reduced it retroactively from cognition, to phrases, to words, to basic letters, and back to the preformal world from which it came. Techniques like *tzeruf,* which interchange "bad" words with "good," helped to remove from thought any notion of permanency.

Having completed the "building" phase, the disciple embarked on the *hakhanot,* or preparations for prayer. This included centering the mind on God, cleansing the body, dressing in non-woolen garments, and putting on a special belt to demarcate the animal from the spiritual self. After taking a pinch of snuff or lighting incense as an aid to concentration, the Hasid prostrated himself on the ground, spread his hands and lifted them toward heaven, then bowed his face between his knees. If he stood to pray, he often swayed—as much to drive off the intrusive thoughts as to express his intensity. Rebbe Zeev Wolf of Zhitomer opposed this habit of swaying: "The Hasid," he said, "should allow the thought of the majesty and greatness of the *En Sof* to enter his mind . . . without any movements of the limbs to push away strange thoughts."

When the Maggid prayed, he saw light emanating from the words of the prayer book, one word shining into the next, the whole fusing with "the universes on high." Rebbe Shneur Zalman, his disciple, saw colors when he sang the *niggun,* a wordless Hasidic chant for inducing ecstasy. "The three colors of white [*Loving-kindness*], red [*Judgment*], and green [*Beauty*] can be expressed in melody." Consequently, he divided the mystical ascent into stages which were to be entered into with an accompanying melody. To effect states of *hishtaphut hanefesh* (outpowering of the soul), *hitorerut* (spiritual awakening), and *hitpaalut* (ecstasy), Shneur Zalman composed a four-bar melody called "The Rebbe's Song," still used today by Lubavitcher Hasidim in their contemplation.

Rebbe Aaron of Karlin (1736–72), "the pioneer of Hasidism in Lithuania," went even further, declaring that singing and dancing were equal to study and meditation. The saintly Levi Isaac of Berdichev composed passionate hymns of praise while rapt in prayer:

> *Where I wander—You!*
> *Where I ponder—You!*
> *Only You everywhere, You, always You.*
> *You, You, You.*
> *When I am gladdened—You!*
> *And when I am saddened—You!*
> *Only You, everywhere You!*
> *You, You, You.*
> *Sky is You!*
> *Earth is You!*
> *You above! You below!*
> *In every trend, at every end,*
> *Only You, everywhere You!*[4]

Like the Lurianic Kabbalists, the Hasidim were very taken with the idea of man as God's necessary helpmate. Since the Absolute had constricted itself for man's sake, it was obligatory for man to purify the entire material world so that the light of the *En Sof* could again radiate without the obstructions cast by illusion. The Hasid never doubted that his separation from God was illusory, nor that his role in life consisted of stripping away the illusion. The ecstatic experience itself became his weapon for penetrating the barrier between his bodily and spiritual selves; *mohin degadlut* (expanded consciousness) was his vehicle to God. Because even the sacred Tetragrammaton had fallen into the material world, it was his duty to purify it, too. Therefore, the Hasid who made of himself a channel for the divine influx, merely by eating, dressing, sleeping, and performing all other daily physical acts, drew the animal, mineral, and vegetable kingdoms back to God.

---

[4] Quoted in H. Rabinowicz, *The World of Hasidism*, pp. 53–54.

One who perceived the Torah stripped of words reunited God and His Name. For such a *tzaddik* not even the physical enactment of the commandments was necessary, for he lived in them, embodied them with his every breath.

Lesser men used the temporal commandments as constricted by space and time. A worthy Hasid who enacted a physical commandment caused a unifying impulse to reverberate throughout the cosmos and thus brought himself and all creation a little closer to the Absolute. There were Hasidic masters who advocated meditating on the "delicious taste" of the Creator with every morsel of a man's favorite food. Others instructed their disciples to picture themselves plunging into flames for the sanctification of God's name. After the Baal Shem Tov's death the more ascetic-minded Hasidim actually returned to the model of their medieval German namesakes and indulged in equally extravagant mortifications. Exercises like visualizing oneself flayed alive were seen as cures for enjoyment of food or sex and as goads to ecstatic fervor. Too much emphasis on the *bad* thoughts and husks of matter embodying the soul resulted in extreme self-chastisement. To eradicate stubbornness, laziness, envy, and the like, certain schools of Hasidim went about mumbling formulas like, "The Canaanite, the Hittite, the Amorite, the Perizzite, the Hivite, the Yebusite, and the Girgashite"—their symbolic counterparts.

"Do not look outside your immediate four cubits," one master warned, "and if you are walking outside and encounter a woman . . . picture God's [feminine] name "Adonai" before your eyes."

Many ascetic Hasidim refrained from talking. In a return to the stricter Lurianic codes, they prayed over everything, from getting up in the morning and evacuating to taking off their clothes at night. The generation of Hasidic masters who followed after the death of the Baal Shem Tov exerted harsh disciplines against distraction in the study hall, even going so far as to extract confessions from their disciples about their most intimate thoughts and to intrude on their marital duties. Penitence became the watchword where joy had once reigned. As one Hasid put it: "Man was created in this physical world only to break down his instincts." The dour and guilty vision that characterized much of early nineteenth-century Hasidism was a far cry from the free and life-asserting proclamations of the Baal Shem Tov and the blissful singing of Levi of Berdichev. Man's natural functions were no longer an emblem of God, but a foul necessity: "The instant you feel that you must move your bowels, you will do so and not allow the excrement to remain inside you and pollute your brain . . . Do not defile your soul by retaining such stool and urine inside yourself even for a moment." Such an attitude could only lead to the hairsplitting, petty squabbling, and inevitable decay of the movement which followed.

THREE GIANTS

Out of the welter of *tzaddikim* who emerged in the wake of the Baal Shem Tov and the Maggid, three men in particular deserve special attention. Rebbe Nachman of Breslov, great-grandson of the Baal Shem Tov, was a wandering Hasid who gave enlightening discourses on meditation anywhere he happened to find himself. Shneur Zalman of Liadi, a formidable scholar, the Maggid's own chief disciple, singlehandedly created a philosophy of Hasidism. And Dov Baer of Lubavitch, Shneur Zalman's son, codified the ecstasy upon which the movement rested.

A true scion of the Baal Shem Tov's family tree, Rebbe Nachman of Breslov, the most hopeful, cheerful, and optimistic of Hasidim, was born on April 4, 1772, in Medzibozh, the town where his great-grandfather had held court. His mother was the daughter of the Baal Shem Tov's saintly daughter; his father, one of the master's leading disciples. At thirteen, Nachman was married to the daughter of a prominent rabbi who gave the young couple a home for the first five years of their wedded life. Even at this tender age Rebbe Nachman had attracted a following of his own, many of whom accompanied him when, at the death of his mother-in-law, he moved his household to Medvedevka. There he preached for ten years, attracting more Hasidim, and gathering around himself a particularly illustrious circle of disciples. His tenure in Medvedevka interrupted by a mysterious pilgrimage to the Holy Land and a feud with a prominent opponent of Hasidism, Rebbe Nachman next made his home in Breslov, his final stopping place. Here, on September 3, 1802, he had a fateful meeting with Rabbi Nathan, a weathy businessman's son who became an instant admirer and who was to be his lifelong companion and scribe. Rebbe Nachman was then thirty; Rabbi Nathan, twenty-two. Though his family disapproved of the connection, Rabbi Nathan gave up his business pursuits to sit at the feet of his teacher. At Rebbe Nachman's order, he alphabetized the major tenets of the Breslov school and indexed the master's discourses for the use of the Breslover Hasidim who were to remain leaderless thereafter. It is for this reason that, even today, the Breslover Hasidim are called the "Dead Hasidim." Rabbi Nathan's manuscript, a full and accurate record of Rebbe Nachman's teachings, was completed in 1805 and published soon after as *Lekutey Moharan* (Sayings of the Master). The key to the book is Nachman's famous doctrine of *hitbodedut,* meditation which could be practiced informally—anywhere, at any time.

Having contracted tuberculosis and sure of his oncoming death, Rebbe Nachman asked his disciples to remove him to Uman, the scene of a recent pogrom, for he wished, he said, to accompany the souls of the martyred Jews with the *tikkunim* (corrections) made by his own death. Maintaining his active teaching schedule to the last, the thirty-eight-year-old Rebbe Nachman died in Uman as he had wished, in 1811. Rabbi Nathan recorded each phase of the master's death with as much love and care as he had lavished on the teachings themselves:

We laid him on the bed, dressed in his fine silk robe. He told [Rabbi] Shimon to arrange his clothes and button his sleeves so that his shirt should not protrude from the robe . . . He took a small ball of wax and rolled it between his fingers, as he often did toward his last days when thinking deep thoughts. Even in this last hour his thoughts were flying through awesome worlds, and he rolled this ball of candlewax between his fingers with great lucidity of mind. The house was filled with many people who had come to honor him . . .

It was not long before he passed away and was gathered to his fathers in great holiness and purity. Bright and clear, he passed away without any confusion whatsoever, without a single untoward gesture, in a state of awesome calmness.[5]

REBBE NACHMAN'S CONVERSATIONS WITH GOD

Although he emphasized joyful and spontaneous meditation above all else, Rebbe Nachman had begun his career with severe fasting that eventually affected his throat and weakened his constitution. Concealing these childhood "devotions" from his family, he nevertheless managed to study the Talmud, Bible, *Zohar*, and Lurianic Kabbalah. While still a youth, he exhibited the power of total recall in his study of the Torah, but experienced great difficulty in comprehending mishnaic and talmudic legalism. For years, he secluded himself and engaged in fervent chanting and prayer, first reciting only the introductory verses of the Psalms and then crying out in wordless prayer to God. These "personal conversations" became the mainstay of his contemplative practices.

Young Nachman hid his religious preoccupations well; he skated on the village pond in winter, played games with boys his age, and became something of a star athlete. But in his very private life, he forced himself to sit for hours in protracted concentration, thinking, "I only have this one day. I will ignore tomorrow and all future days. I only have this one

5 All quotations relating to Rebbe Nachman are from Aryeh Kaplan, translator, *Rabbi Nachman's Wisdom*.

day alone." Continued mental and physical exertions of this sort eventually resulted in his acquisition of supernormal powers. As he told his disciples later:

> Every man can attain the highest level. It depends on nothing but your own free choice. You must truly care about yourself and carefully decide what good truly lies before you . . . The main thing is prayer. Accustom yourself to beg and plead before God. Speak to Him in any language you understand—this is especially important. Beg Him to open your eyes. Ask Him to help you along the path of devotion. Plead that you be worthy of drawing close to Him.

His trip to the Holy Land added a further dimension of spirituality to Rebbe Nachman's exalted condition. It was apparent to the disciples from the moment he returned that the master had indeed achieved new levels of ecstasy never seen by them before. "His vision knew no bounds," wrote Rabbi Nathan. And from that point on Nachman preached the realization of "ignorance": "No matter how high one reaches, there is still the next step. Therefore, we never know anything, and still do not attain the true goal. This is a very deep and mysterious concept." Rebbe Nachman evidently saw the perilous voyage to the Holy Land as a living metaphor of his own dramatic expansion of consciousness—it had taught him how little he actually knew. So strongly did the importance of "ignorance" seem that he began denouncing all philosophical speculation as a pale shadow of the Torah's intuitive powers. He exhorted his Hasidim to give up all desire for wealth, intellectual knowledge, beauty, and other possessions. Worldly pleasures, he said, were "like sunbeams in a dark room. They may actually seem solid, but one who tries to grasp a sunbeam finds nothing in his hand."

Once cleansed of desire, the Breslover Hasid could approach the meditation of joy. "Foolishness," said Rebbe Nachman, could elevate a man to bliss; "screaming in silence" gave him a direct line to God:

You can shout loudly in a "small still voice" [1 Kings 19:12] without anyone hearing you . . . Anyone can do this. Just imagine the sound of such a scream in your mind. Depict the shout in your imagination, exactly as it would sound. Keep this up until you are . . . screaming in this soundless "small still voice." This is actually a scream and not mere imagination. Just as some vessels bring the sound from your lungs to your lips, others bring it to the brain. You can draw the sound through these nerves, literally bringing it into your head. When you do this, you are actually shouting inside your brain. You can stand in a crowded room, screaming in this manner, with no one able to hear you. Sometimes when you do this, a sound may escape your lips. The voice, traveling through the nerves, can also activate the vocal organs, which might produce some very faint sound . . . It is much easier to shout this way without words. When you wish to express words, it is much more difficult to hold the voice in the mind without allowing any sound to escape. But without words it is much easier.

In order to perform such concentrated "conversations with God," the Breslover Hasid trained himself to "forget" his business, his current and past experiences, his household affairs, and any real or imagined transgressions he had committed. Immediately after an event had occurred, he checked it from ever again intruding on his mind. Living entirely in the present moment was all the Rebbe ever demanded of the disciple in the way of "mortification," for Nachman never forgot the depressions he had endured as a result of his own youthful asceticism. Experience had taught him how ruinous such practices could be to the Hasid's health. Only *hitbodedut*, he felt, could successfully show a man that his "true face is his mind, which illuminates it from within."

The most subtle of all Hasidic psychologists, Rebbe Nachman differentiated between "heartbreak" and "depression," as spiritual yearning and splenetic self-indulgence, respectively. He instructed his disciples to set aside a specific amount of time each day for "heartbreak periods," devoted to meeting

God in total self-abnegation and longing. Further to keep them from confusing longing with depression, he defined the latter as an angry complaint against God and compared it to a child's temper tantrum. On the other hand, the disciple might, if he wished, regard himself as a child who found itself far from its father and longed with a broken heart to be reunited with him. This was the safe way which could do no harm to the mind, the Hasid's precious implement for "penetrating the loftiest heights."

Rebbe Nachman continuously extolled the powers of the concentrated mind:

> One who does not meditate cannot have Wisdom. He may occasionally be able to concentrate, but not for any length of time. His power of concentration remains weak and cannot be maintained. One who does not meditate also does not realize the foolishness of the world. But one who has a relaxed and penetrating mind can see that it is all vanity.

Like other Jewish masters, he, too, strongly believed that thoughts could actually influence events in the physical world. But unlike the others, Rebbe Nachman enjoined his disciples to concentrate on spiritual impulses so strongly as to make them come true. He advised them to become literally obsessed with the desire for *devekuth*. Directed at the heart, this attitude was called "God's counsel." Perfect attention to each word of prayer recited while concentrating on the heart meant emphasizing each letter and visualizing oneself as a limb of the cosmic man. Whenever a specific part of the liturgy moved him to ecstasy, the Hasid knew that he had touched the limb from which his soul had come. When the ecstasy faded and the words grew flat, he knew that he had left his soul's "root":

> All of your future life is determined by what you find during the time of exploration. If you are worthy of more time in which the lamps created by your deeds shine, you will certainly find more good in the King's treasury. It all depends on how long your lamp can burn.

Like the Ari, Rebbe Nachman also took full responsibility for his Hasidim, going so far as to prescribe specific spiritual remedies for each man. His followers believed that he also shared the Ari's ability to read faces. Nachman himself claimed to know the degree of a person's spiritual perception from that person's opening words. Nachman claimed he could recognize a lustful person from the shape of his nose and the purity of a Hasid's faith from the configuration of his feet. Simpler than the Ari in his demands, Nachman encouraged his disciples to perform piously in their everyday dealings. Rather than elaborate *yichudim,* he appointed only certain Hasidim to prolonged meditation and others to a vegetarian diet. All of his students, however, were compelled to read the *Shulkhan Aruch* (legal code) daily. He was flexible enough to permit unlearned Hasidim to pray out in the meadows, and encouraged them to communicate with God in their native tongues when they could not speak Hebrew. For Rebbe Nachman, speaking from the depths of the heart was aways far more important than exhibiting scholarship.

Each physical movement made during the day was an emblem of the Hasid's surrender to God. The Breslover condensed all of his being into a desire for truth by indulging in imaginary dialogues with his soul: *What will become of you? What will you do in the end? What will you answer the One who sent you? What do you think? What are you on earth if not a stranger? What is your life if not vanity and emptiness? You know this well. What do you say?*

Under the skillful guidance of the master, the Breslover Hasid turned these questions over and over in his mind until they had penetrated his soul. After prolonged meditation he confronted the truth behind the questions: there was no escape from the world's suffering except through the path of the Torah. Rebbe Nachman assured him that he was correct, that even the pagan philosophers had concluded thus. "But," he added, "if you wish to turn your back on it and remain immersed in the deep quicksand of this world, there is no one to prevent you."

Kabbalah

REBBE SHNEUR ZALMAN:
THE INTELLECTUAL MYSTIC

The direct antithesis to Rebbe Nachman's democratic assertion that, with the proper meditative training and devotion, all men could become *tzaddikim,* was Rebbe Shneur Zalman's declaration that true *tzaddikim* were born and not made. This Russian intellectual, prized disciple of the Maggid and founder of his own sect, amplified the Lurianic Kabbalah in the Hasidic context. Born in 1747 in Liozno, in central Russia, Shneur Zalman was a brilliant child prodigy, with a particular talent for traversing the convoluted mazes of talmudic logic. But instead of studying with the great Gaon of Vilna, the natural choice for a talmudic genius, the young Russian scholar opted for the mystical Maggid of Mezerich. The master immediately instructed his new charge to write a mystical reinterpretation of the *Shulkhan Aruch,* which Shneur Zalman completed by the time he was twenty-five. He further added to his Hasidic studies by enrolling as a student of Menachem Mendel of Vitebsk who, together with the Maggid, was then disseminating the Baal Shem Tov's original teachings. At this time, too, Shneur Zalman embarked upon his own philosophical opus, *Tanya* (an acronym of the book's full title), which took him twenty years to complete.

With the fight between the rationalist *Mitnaggedim* and the Hasidim at its peak, the ailing Maggid sent Shneur Zalman and Menachem Mendel to intercede with the Gaon of Vilna, who was then threatening to issue an excommunicative ban on the ecstatic sect. Shneur Zalman's reputation as a talmudist, he thought, would surely open the door to a reconciliation. The Gaon, however, was so dead set against the Hasidim that he did not even permit the two scholars to enter beyond his front hall. Shortly thereafter the dread ban was pronounced, and the war between mystics and rationalists officially began. This did not deter Shneur Zalman from publishing his *Tanya* in 1796 when the fighting was at its height. Menachem Mendel soon after journeyed to the Holy Land with a group of disciples; when he received a copy of his friend's book he was aghast. Shneur Zalman, he felt, had completely misinterpreted the Baal Shem Tov's teachings; *Tanya* was too "kabbalistic" for the average Hasid—the book would have to be destroyed. Thus ensued the second schism, this one between the Hasidim themselves—a break which to this day has isolated the Lubavitcher sect of Shneur Zalman from all the others. Enemies of all stripes eventually persuaded the Gentile Russian authorities to imprison Shneur Zalman as a spy. But all charges were dropped and he was released after several months and eventually permitted to settle in Liadi, where he became the leader of an assortment of Jewish mystical and political groups.

Since he believed that "the ordinary man is in conflict with his animal nature, and it is only the true *tzaddik* who overcomes his animal soul completely," Shneur Zalman helped to elevate the Hasidic master to exalted levels. Even now his Lubavitcher descendants, reputed miracle men, rule with a strong hand over hundreds of thousands of loyal Hasidim who submit their wills to the decisions of the *tzaddik,* their Rebbe. The Lubavitcher dynasty was further enhanced by its traditional father–son succession. Residing in Brooklyn, today's Rebbe is a son-in-law of the previous Rebbe, a direct descendant of Shneur Zalman himself.

Perhaps because of his naturally intellectual bent, Shneur Zalman chose to emphasize the "knowledge" aspect of enlightenment. Unlike the Baal Shem Tov, who advocated simple devotion, he focused on *hasagah* (intellect) as the means to *devekuth.* The Lubavitcher invoked *Knowledge,* the secret sphere on the cosmic tree as a contemplative phase during which the mind connected itself to the "idea" of God before transmitting it to the emotional centers. *Wisdom* represented the initial flash of divine consciousness; *Understanding* conditioned it for reflection on a physical level. Where other Kabbalists had started contemplation with the seven lower spheres, Shneur Zalman characteristically went right to the brain. *Habad*, as he called his system, is a name culled from the first Hebrew letters of the spheres designating *Wisdom* (*Hokhmah*) *Understanding* (*Binah*), and *Knowledge* (*Daath*), which is located invisibly between the first two. *Knowledge*, the fluid intermediary between body and idea, motivated the Hasid toward the two higher states of consciousness and simultaneously helped him to "climb" there.

Returning to the cosmic tree of spheres, the Habad Hasidim virtually ignored the letters of prayer. Shneur Zalman's scheme of visual and intellectual contemplation consisted of reflecting on God's omniscience, imagining his own soul as a spark issuing from a great flame until he was no longer conscious of separation between himself and the idea upon which he concentrated (a state called *tevunah*). The Lubavitcher Rebbe suggested concentrating first on created beings, for they were easier to encompass in images. More advanced meditation consisted of reflection on the Nothingness from which those created beings had emerged. "Joy" came with the feeling of God's closeness; "sorrow" at the sense of His remoteness. If his soul truly yearned to bridge the space between itself and the apparently inaccessible Creator, the Habad Hasid compressed all "illusory" spheres into one light. The ecstasy induced as a result of this visualization Shneur Zalman called *hitlahavut* and the rapture following contemplative prayer, *hitpaalut*.

Like his master the Maggid, Shneur Zalman also believed God's invisibility to be an illusion wrought by man's ignorance. The Hasid's best means for breaking the spell was consciously to motivate his soul by means of the breath to which it was tied: "When someone breathes, he does so from within himself, from his innermost being. When a person breathes with force, he makes use of his essential power and innermost being." In his book for average spiritual seekers, *Sefer Shel Benonim*, Shneur Zalman recommended meditation on the undivided Absolute without the usual attendant references to spheres and states of mind. He warned, however, that merely grasping the idea of God's greatness was only part of the process, that only experiential awareness of Him could replace wishful fantasizing that might pass for ecstasy. Ritual became the Hasid's restraining rod, a prerequisite for the annihilation of the ego that must precede the mystic union: "So long as the animal soul serves as a vehicle for the divine soul, as it is meant to do, there is complete unity and harmony; the moment the animal soul acts independently, the harmony is disturbed." Only sustained contemplation could awaken the divine intelligence that resides in every soul. And only the divine intelligence could advance one toward *Wisdom*, "the recognition of the unreality of matter as perceived by the senses, including the complete suspension of the self and its merging into the Divine All." Continued refinement of the animal self by means of contemplation involving the divine intelligence, would ultimately efface the illusory veil of matter separating man from his divine source, for at this level the human soul was literally part of the Absolute.

SUBDUING THE ANIMAL SELF

Work on the animal self had to be performed on its own terms. According to Shneur Zalman, meritorious action was one way to chip it down; prayer was another: "During sincere and ecstatic prayer, the animal . . . is mesmerized . . . All thoughts of the flesh are banished . . ." The Hasid who still harbored "natural" tendencies could not be considered perfect. For this reason, the Lubavitcher Rebbe prescribed observing the commandments as a means of liberating the divine sparks from their captors, the material husks which enclose all animal, vegetable, and mineral life. Moreover, when multiplied by the performance of many "ordinary" Hasidim, these spark-liberating acts were continually "spiritualizing" the entire physical world. The sign that he had perfectly enacted the ritual was the Hasid's ecstatic glimpse into the Sinai mystery.

Nonetheless, the Rebbe said, "the same creative force . . . that is responsible for the existence of the good and the holy is also responsible for the bad and the unholy." Acknowledging this, the Habad Hasid ignored the didactic aspect of the commandments and emphasized their suprarational quality instead. Torah study, for example, meant joining the human and divine intellect on physical ground. In this way, *thought,* the soul's "food," brought the soul nourishment by the study of scripture. Physical cleansing once having subdued the desires of the Hasid's animal self, the soul was free to soar in mystic flight to its origin. The best "physical" act, said Shneur Zalman, was benevolence toward one's fellow beings. But prayer was even less corruptible since it was "strictly a matter between the worshiper and his Maker." The Rebbe instructed his Hasidim on no account to pray *for* anything, but to use the liturgy as a tool for self-analysis. The word *hitpalel* (to pray), he reminded them, also meant "to judge oneself." Liberation of the soul thus became the Hasid's daily experience. Symbolized as "liberation from Egypt," the prayers performed three times daily unlocked the divine soul from its material casings. (*Mitzraim,* the Hebrew name for Egypt, with a shift in vowel points, becomes *metzarim* [limitations].) Having learned to delight in this "exodus," the Hasid sought to repeat it, making it a permanent state, which he called *Shabbat* (Perfection), or Sabbath. So he read the experience metaphorically into the days of the week as well. The Rebbe taught his disciple that the task of his weekdays was to "build" for himself a tabernacle by means of good deeds, thoughtful speech, and God-directed thinking. On the Sabbath, however, he was to refrain from all "building," retreat into the tabernacle, and dwell in holiness "without Egypt"—material limitations.

BUILDING THE PERFECT "SHABBAT"

Only perfect concentration, performed by a stable intellect, a humbled ego, and a yearning heart, could build the perfect

Shabbat. Nevertheless, urged Shneur Zalman, "one is not commanded to excite emotions that are not there, but to awaken and cultivate a natural and deeply rooted attachment."

Always practical, the Rebbe refrained from attributing negative traits to matter. Man used it, was indeed composed of it; his object was to infuse it with so much spirit that it reflected God. Nature's qualities—activity, inertia, and perfect equilibrium—were helpful in provoking lazy minds and bodies or quieting overly active ones. There were no mortifications in the Habad training, none of the condemnations of natural bodily functions that marked many contemporary Hasidic sects. Instead, transforming lust into love, the Lubavitcher disciple planted his yearning at the right side of his heart, away from the left ventricle, symbolic home of "sensory" desires, and allowed his soul to melt into the Infinite: "for this is its will and desire by its nature."

DOV BAER OF LUBAVITCH: THE TEN STAGES OF ECSTASY

Shneur Zalman's unremitting monism was even further augmented by his son, Dov Baer (1774–1827). Like the Maggid, his adored namesake, Dov Baer of Lubavitch subscribed to the idea that "there is nothing else apart from God since all is in God." This "panentheistic" philosophy (different from pantheism, which sees God in everything) spurred him to distinguish between "physical" and "spiritual" ecstasy. His belief in levels of spiritual accomplishment, personified by "ladders" of the soul, resulted in Dov Baer's division of ecstasy into ten stages, five occurring in the animal soul and five in the divine.

Assuming his father's post as leader of the Habad Hasidim, Dov Baer did not meet with full acceptance. Rebbe Aaron of Staroselye, one of his father's leading disciples, attacked what he called Dov Baer's "intellectual" style of contemplation as follows:

> If there is to be contemplation on His unity, blessed be He, and His attachment to the worlds . . . there must first be that

type of contemplation which consists only in reflection on the majesty of the King . . . I have dwelt on this matter at some length because there are many who have turned from the reasonable way and have derived from this teaching the idea that the only thing which matters is contemplation alone without any awakening of the heart whatsoever.[6]

According to Rebbe Aaron, Shneur Zalman, the "Elder Rebbe," had allowed his Hasidim at least the illusion of Love if he felt they were not yet ready to contemplate Nothingness. It was as if, after allowing a glimpse of a personal God, the leader of the movement had changed his mind and quickly stolen it away again. Regardless of his father's apparent indulgence toward a "God with form," Dov Baer was determined to replace it with Nothingness. He rebuked his Hasidim for using this indulgence to evoke "ecstasy," which he regarded as spiritual self-titillation. This was not the way, "for when one exerts himself with many devices to attain this state . . . if he experiences it, he rejoices with the ardor of his enthusiasm . . . and if it does not come, he becomes depressed. This . . . is the source of great confusion."

The years of Dov Baer's leadership were already reflecting the artificially induced ecstasies bordering on hysteria that had begun to characterize the decay of the Hasidic movement. To stem this, he exhorted his followers to turn their meditation away from experience of ecstasy and toward the Divine. Habad contemplation now focused on the idea that "All is God" to the exclusion of everything else. Hence, the divine No-thing could only be experienced by an equally "no-thinged" man and not a "blissful" one. To teach this emptying technique, Dov Baer compiled his *Tract on Ecstasy,* published sometime after 1814.

Opening with the uncompromising declaration that "There is no reality in created things . . . from the point of view of the divine vitality which sustains us, we have no existence

[6] From Introduction, Dov Baer of Lubavitch, *Tract on Ecstasy,* pp. 44–45.

. . . From which it follows that there is no other existence
whatsoever apart from His existence . . . ," Dov Baer points
to desire for experience of the Divine as the first step on the
road to truth. Ecstasy of this type, according to Dov Baer, the
"Middle Rebbe," consists of "loving" and is experienced in the
physical heart. The intellectual wish to know God, he called
"hearing from afar." From here, the Hasid progressed to "natural fear," the point at which he decided to alter his life style
in accord with his search for unity. This phase frequently
made him feel inadequate and prompted him to withdraw
from the material world. The committed disciple, though
clearing his path of "obstacles" by shunning temporal achievements, had "been moved only to ecstasy in thought, not, as
yet, to ecstasy of heart at all." But he could take joy in worship and perform charitable acts in the knowledge that he
would be drawing closer to God each time he sat in meditation.

Ecstasy of the heart announced itself as a deep and vital
sense of the Absolute—but still wrapped in the "garment" of
one's animal self. Only great mental effort could provoke intellectual "love" and "fear" from the animal self, the two prereq-
uisites to higher consciousness being represented by the
spheres of *Loving-kindness* and *Judgment* on the contemplative map of the tree. Finally, "simple will" transcended
both the animal and intellectual selves and elevated the Hasid
to the secret sphere of *Knowledge*. Those with more highly
developed souls would achieve more expanded degrees of
spiritual *Knowledge*. The man with even the merest trace of
ego would see the Divine as existing outside of himself. If he
purified his animal self through absorption in the Torah's
precepts, the Hasid would quite naturally awaken the divine
soul, whose very nature it is to elevate matter.

Exhibiting traditional Hasidic sensitivity to psychology,
Dov Baer matched meditative subjects with individual per-
sonalities. For some disciples he prescribed contemplation of
their own "lowliness"; for others he recommended meditation

on their "closeness" to God. Regardless of the mode, he stressed spontaneity, comparing the liberation of the soul to a lightning flash. True ecstasy, he said, was "not something which follows on intellectual perception but is identical with it." Even the awareness of loving disappeared in Dov Baer's brand of ecstasy, which was wordless. That is why the "simple song" composed by his father had no words, only the "essence" of melody itself, like the ecstasy which transcended reasonable thought. Pure sound represented a state more exalted than the sacred form of the letters. In the pure blast of the *shofar*, his disciple would find "the simple sound which proceeds from the breath of the heart." Greater than reason, higher than speech which, like reason, is derived from the brain, greater than the false "ecstasy" of the physical heart is the "higher will" embodied in pure sound. Ideally, the man whose refined animal nature and lofty divine soul had united in partnership would be "successful in all the divine goodness," ready to absorb in himself the primordial sound of which the universe was made.

Habad Hasidim regarded visionary experiences as "delusions of the blood," self-induced images resulting from an overexcited imagination. Dov Baer instead emphasized the importance of an exercise he called "looking"—that is, investigating concrete objects so that they made a lasting impression on the mind, examining even the slightest detail until the Hasid knew it so well that he had become one with its "essence." Still higher than this was a stage he called "probing," where one surpassed even *Wisdom* by tracing an idea to its source. The purpose of these exercises in contemplation was "to observe indeed that the variety of existence is only an 'appearance' and that the ultimate reality is undivided and One. . . . Reflection on these details is not to be confined to those of the physical world. It includes meditation on the whole [tree of spheres] and the coordination of all the higher worlds."

The discrepancy between the Habad school of Hasidism

and the Baal Shem Tov's "simple prayer" is personified by
both the "Elder" and "Middle" Rebbes' return to the highly intellectual path of spheres. The Baal Shem Tov's followers for
the most part ignored the ordinary meaning of the liturgy and
created their "unifications" from the non-rational phrases
which appeared to them during ecstasy. Indeed, most Hasidic
masters chastised the Habad Rebbes for reverting to esoteric
methods that no longer suited the needs or capacities of the
common folk who constituted their flocks. Dwelling strictly on
the vital power of the letters, they felt, was sufficient for the
masses. Over the objections of their colleagues, Shneur Zalman and Dov Baer restored the role of the intellect in Jewish
mystical practice. The Baal Shem Tov, too, could provide arduous meditative techniques for his inner circle when they were
called for, but his public teachings continually placed devotional and ecstatic prayer ahead of mental exercises—the
heart ahead of the mind. Unlike Shneur Zalman, he did not
choose to speak for a superior breed of men whose mental
elasticity and moral purity approached the Absolute without
a tear, a sigh, or a groan. Yet Shneur Zalman's elite Habad
system was more in touch with the needs of the coming times,
for the Lubavitcher Hasidim are the only branch of the movement still thriving today. And the Baal Shem Tov has receded
into legend.

III
Devekuth: Cleaving to God

6
The Way of God

Within the realm of perfect mental functioning acquired through *devekuth*, or cleaving to God, lay prophecy, communication with celestial messengers, and power over natural laws. Attaining spiritual perfection was synonymous for the Jewish mystic with returning to his source, or "root." The more he resembled God, the vaster his mental power and compassion. Paradoxically, Jewish masters taught that it was man's very lowliness, his physicality, which would help to elevate him. With the Torah and rituals to subdue his desires, the mystic had a head start. Next, confronting each level of his soul in succession, he discovered that what he had initially considered his "identity" was really a ladder of smaller selves, with the "divine soul," or "intelligence," at the top. Each descending rung was bound to the one below it. The last, or animal self, of which the mystic was conscious in waking life, was in turn linked to the blood of the physical body. Five stages comprised the Kabbalist's journey through his soul:

1. Animal Nature
2. Spiritual Nature
3. Breath
4. Living Essence
5. Unique Essence, or Union.

According to Jewish philosophers, the lowest levels of the soul's ladder are experienced by ordinary people in sleep.

While all outer faculties are at rest, the imagination continues to function. Images created in the mind are a mixture of daily residue or the result of physiological processes like digestion and blood pressure. Dreams, the result of these combined factors, are thus the average person's claim to "prophecy," for they represent the work of imagination, the highest faculty of the animal nature.

More spiritually developed people, dominated by the intellectual level of the soul, will dream of moving about in the celestial realm, where they communicate with disembodied beings they call "angels." When these "journeys" are transmitted to the animal nature, whose image-making function turns them into dreams, the individual may obtain significant messages from the celestial realm. He must be careful, for the information is often mixed with subjective wishes and distortions stemming from his own emotional life. The Jewish sages have always therefore warned that it is impossible for the average person to have a real prophetic dream without a considerable admixture of worthless information.

Kabbalists who uttered God's Names and altered their breathing patterns were making use of the third rung of the soul's ladder, the breath which tied them to the spiritual world. By binding himself mentally to a specific "spiritual being," the Kabbalist could either elevate himself further (as Abulafia taught) or he could obtain significant information about the future. This second practice was dangerous, for it often resulted in making contact with *shedim,* demonic beings who altered and confused the meditator's mind. Along this path lay the danger of insanity. The "breath," or third level of soul, was therefore regarded as a two-edged sword. Only utmost purity of purpose assured the Kabbalist safe passage to the next rung. But spontaneous ecstasy could occur here, too —a condition in which the mystic, without any conscious effort, might find himself flooded with a rush of divine bliss. Yet even this level of "divine inspiration" was not really considered true "prophecy."

PROPHECY

The prophet's spiritual nature worked toward *devekuth* of such permanence that he became clearly and consciously certain of his oneness with the Absolute at all times. Like Moses, the true prophet required no angels, no intermediaries of any kind. The greater his spiritual development, the more calm and quiet his mental and physical condition. Minor prophets lost consciousness at the peak of their trances, but the perfect prophet cleaved undistractedly to his source even in the midst of his tumultuous daily affairs. This highest level of *devekuth*, occurring at the fifth stage of the soul, was called *yechidah*, the perfect union with the Absolute.

Language, prayer, and chanting were only vehicles for first visualizing and then annihilating oneself in God.

Oddly enough, it was the rationalist philosopher Maimonides who drew up the qualifications for true prophetic experience. First, he said, the devotee had to be in perfect neurological and psychological condition; physical fortitude came next. Unlike other mystics, Maimonides emphasized, prophets were always highly intellectual, rational men equipped to discriminate between hallucination and actual transcendental experience. Ascetic to the point where he had relinquished all ambition but the desire to know God, the prophet was free of wish-fulfilling visions. Nor would he ever enter the prophetic state in a mournful, angry, or distracted mood.

Maimonides further went on to say that once the prophet had drawn down the *shefa* (divine influx), he was transformed into an earth-dwelling "angel"—a superhuman man who had risen even above the level of the greatest Jewish sages. At this point he assumed a social function, usually rising up and founding a nation, or instructing the masses according to the divine plan. He did not have to perform miracles to prove himself; the obvious test for the efficacy or falsehood of his prophecy, according to Maimonides, was that the enlightened prophet's predictions (unlike those of astrologers and fortune tellers) *always* came true.

Abraham Abulafia failed in his attempts to revive the prophetic mode in Jewish mystical practice. The habits and meditative techniques of the biblical "Sons of the Prophets" are only vaguely suggested in the prophetic books of the Old Testament, and we can only guess at what went on in these ancient organized schools for Jewish mystics. The life style of the Essene community at Qumran hints at the ascetic and somewhat isolated life of the prophets, but only Maimonides, more than thirteen centuries later, was willing to define prophecy for sure.

SUPERNATURAL GUIDES

What the enlightened mystic actually experienced at the time of his *devekuth,* the moment of his cleaving to God, is better documented in the sixteenth-century experience of Joseph Caro. One of the most fascinating phenomena in Jewish mystical life was the appearance to certain Kabbalists of a supernatural guide. The word *"maggid"* means "one who relates," and, in ordinary life, denoted an itinerant preacher (cf. the Maggid of Mezerich). The celestial *maggid,* however, dictated messages through the Kabbalist's mouth, and in his own voice. From the sixteenth through eighteenth centuries, the evocation of *maggidim* became the mark of the spiritually blessed. Jacob of Marvège, a Provençal Kabbalist, even collected a whole manual of "questions for heavenly messengers," which were designed to induce maggidic communication. In sixteenth-century Constantinople, a group of Kabbalists under the direction of Rabbi Joseph Taytazak, made evocation of spiritual guides a group practice.

The most famous *maggid* of all appeared to Joseph Caro, the great rationalist lawyer of Safed who compiled the *Shulkhan Aruch* (legal code), which is the mainstay of normative, anti-mystical Judaism today. Joseph Caro and his fellow citizens of Safed, however, saw no incompatibility between knowing God and serving Him. On Friday nights after synagogue services, large groups of people assembled in Rabbi Caro's home to witness the divine manifestation uttered through his lips as he sat in trance. None saw any contradiction whatsoever in the dual personality of their respected rabbinic authority and saint.

A shade lower than prophecy, *maggidism* enabled the mystic to tap the vast spiritual reservoir of saints and sages, the realm of Elijah, and sometimes even the essence of the embodied scriptures. At times, for example, Caro's *maggid* called itself *Sovereignty*, the tenth sphere, or immanent presence of the Absolute in our world. When Caro meditated on the Mishnah (Oral Law) or Gemarrah (Commentaries on the Scripture), the *maggid* appeared to him as the "spirit" of Mishnah or Gemarrah.

Two centuries later, Moses Chayim Luzzatto of Padua wrote to a friend about his *maggid*:

> I admit that since 1727 God has been gracious to me by dispatching to me a holy one from heaven who reveals to me . . . nightly secrets . . . he promised me that I would be privileged to hear [the utterances] from the very mouth of the prophet Elijah and even the living words of the Lord. And as he promised, so it came. When the appointed time arrived, the prophet Elijah revealed himself to me, followed by the holy souls who abide on this earth ready to fulfill the tasks of the Lord . . . And with their assistance I composed many and important works.

This had happened after Luzzatto fell asleep while repeating a kabbalistic formula, probably one of the *yichudim* out of the Lurianic prayer book. He was awakened suddenly by a voice, saying in Aramaic: "I came down to reveal hidden secrets of the Holy King." Though trembling with fright, Luzzatto stood and listened as the voice enumerated kabbalistic teachings. Luzzatto made similar preparations in his room the next day, and again the voice came, expounding Kabbalah as before.

This continued for some days at a time until finally the voice confessed to being a *maggid* who promised to provide the young Kabbalist with "certain formulas to keep in mind every day" until he returned. No physical creature ever manifested, only a voice which Luzzatto could hear and feel speaking through his own lips.

Luzzatto's relationship with his *maggid* grew so deep that he could ask questions and receive immediate and pertinent replies. After three months the *maggid* stopped the formulas and, substituting the Holy Name in their place, promised a vision of Elijah. Not surprisingly, Elijah appeared and promised Luzzatto that Metatron, "the great guardian of Heaven," would follow. Elijah proved true to his word, so that shortly after, Luzzatto could confidently report to his diary: "I can recognize each one of them. Also there are holy souls who come, their names I know not, and they tell me new things which I write down . . . All these things I am doing while falling on my face and while seeing the holy souls as if through a dream in human forms."

For three years Luzzatto lived in almost continuous ecstasy. At first he disclosed nothing of the experience to anyone, but when he could no longer hold it back, he confessed his secret to Jekutiel Gordon, a trusted friend. Gordon, a young medical student and devoted member of Luzzatto's kabbalistic circle, took it upon himself to inform the world. Assuming the role of a mystic Boswell, he left the faculty of medicine at the University of Padua in order to devote himself entirely to spreading the word about Luzzatto's enlightenment. Gordon intimated that the *maggid* had designated Luzzatto a spark of Rabbi Akiva's soul, and claimed that it had commanded him to write a new *Zohar*. Other disciples also enthusiastically endorsed the young Kabbalah master, but, like Gordon, they could never admit to hearing a word of the *maggid's* communications themselves. As evidence for its legitimacy, they cited the lofty stream of compositions Luzzatto was turning out at the time of the *maggid's* appearances. Could such mystic treatises be anything but divinely inspired?

Gordon further pleaded Luzzatto's case:

> He also knows all the transmigrations of the souls and the requirements of every man's soul as to purification . . . At first his *Maggid* was permitted to tell him only the secrets of the Torah, but now he tells him everything, and no one knows of it except us, his disciples.[1]

Public justifications like these soon attracted the attention of a certain Rabbi Moses Hagiz, a hardened rationalist on the lookout for dangerous pseudo-Messiahs like Sabbatai Zevi; Luzzatto was just the right target for him. In 1730 Hagiz informed the rabbis of Venice that a self-proclaimed Messiah was living in their midst. For five years the rabbis persecuted the young prophet, spurred on by Hagiz and fought off by the respected Rabbi Isaiah Bassan, Luzzatto's former teacher.

Hounded and finally even excommunicated by the rabbis of Italy and Germany, Luzzatto, now married, moved with his wife and son to Amsterdam. There he lived peacefully, no longer prone to publicizing his visionary experiences—if indeed he had any. Having sworn a written oath never again to teach Kabbalah, Luzzatto soon after removed himself to Palestine, where he succumbed to plague, dying in the town of Tiberius in 1746—his life a testament to the scorn which Jews have traditionally heaped upon their prophets.

THE SECRET DIARY OF JOSEPH CARO

Joseph Caro's *maggid,* appearing more than two hundred years earlier, fared better. The history of that heavenly manifestation appeared unexpectedly in 1646 in a Polish bookseller's shop.

Caro, the purported author of the 160-page account, entitled *Maggid Mesharim,* had died seventy-one years before in

[1] Quoted in Simon Ginzburg, *The Life and Works of Moses Hayyim Luzzatto.*

Safed, Palestine. Nobody ever found out how the book had made its way to Lublin, Poland; but although it conflicted drastically in temper and spirit with the author's other well-known legal treatises, experts agreed that the book was indeed Caro's. The *Maggid Mesharim* was written in the form of a secret diary kept by Caro for a period of fifty-two years, from the ages of thirty-two to eighty-four. In it were included other personal references which pointed to the rich and colorful life of the saintly rabbi. Interspersed between its notes on his three marriages, six children, and various comings and goings were many verbatim discourses between a celestial messenger and Caro himself.

Preferring to appear on the Sabbath (which Caro spent in deep meditation and spiritual study), the *maggid* entered the rabbi's conscious mind and spoke through his mouth on a variety of subjects ranging from personal events in Caro's future and the future of the Jewish community to activities taking place among the departed Jewish saints in paradise. Depending on the form and intensity of Caro's ecstasy, the *maggid's* appearances were as varied as the angels, heavenly attributes, and legal commentaries which dominated his mind during waking consciousness. Since Caro spent so much of his time pondering the Mishnah, the sixty-three-volume compilation of oral law prepared by Judah the Prince in 200 c.e., it is therefore no surprise that his *maggid* would disclose itself to him as the embodied spirit of the Mishnah. Even Caro's induction to meditation was inspired by the spirit of the Mishnah, which agreed to appear, "provided you cleave unto me, unto my Mishnayoth [laws], unto my service, unto my fear, and do not separate your mind from me even for one moment." It further warned him: "There may be wandering thoughts in your mind that interfere and these cause that not all my words come true, and they also cause me to stammer and prevent me from revealing to you everything."[2] Although Caro was himself

[2] Quotations in this section are from *Maggid Mesharim*, 1551 edition, translated by Aryeh Kaplan.

awake and conscious during the *maggid*'s appearances, he would often fall to stammering at the slightest break in concentration, when its words failed to come through his lips.

Outwardly, no special events preceded Joseph Caro's prophetic mediumship. Born in Toledo, Spain, in 1488, he and his family settled in Constantinople at the expulsion of the Jews from Spain. Caro was a man of scholarly disposition, but that did not deter him from marrying three times and fathering a family with his second wife. The *maggid* often referred to this woman, saying that her illustrious kabbalistic ancestors and her own spiritual depth were a powerful influence on Caro's meditative life. But the real turning point came when Caro met Solomon Molko, a Portuguese Marrano mystic then in the Levant, whose eccentric, checkered past had included a dramatic self-circumcision and a dangerous public assertion in Portugal of his Jewish birth. Molko, who harbored messianic notions, was a charismatic figure openly possessing transcendent powers. When the young prophet came to a martyr's end at the Inquisitor's stake in Italy, proclaiming the opening of the Messianic Age, Caro vowed from that day onward to follow in his footsteps. The diary shows that all his life he bore an almost obsessive urge to die as Molko had, a public martyr to the Jewish cause. Destiny was to treat him more gently, for he died peacefully at home in Palestine at the age of eighty-seven, a celebrated rabbinical scholar, codifier of the most illustrious text of Jewish ritual law, and—only in his secret life—a prophet.

While living in Constantinople, Caro fell in with the *maggid*-evoking Rabbi Joseph Taytazak and his circle. A highly respected scholar, mystic, and ascetic, Taytazak studied eighteen hours a day, ate almost nothing, and slept for a few hours, in a painfully convoluted posture, in a narrow wooden box. Despite his powerful influence on the young Kabbalist, Taytazak could not keep Caro from rushing to the Holy Land at the news of Molko's death.

The year was 1536, the mystic community of Safed was in

its heyday; Caro had hurried there to await the incarnation of the Messiah. Caro fit perfectly into the circle of Kabbalists which then included mystic luminaries like Solomon Alkabez and Moses Cordovero. In fact, by the time he was fifty-eight, Caro had so distinguished himself in the community that he was crowned Chief Rabbi of Safed. According to the diary, the *maggid* had already appeared to him while he was studying with Taytazak in Constantinople, advising him to hurry to Safed, where he was sure to fulfill his spiritual destiny. "Go to the Holy Land," it said, "because not all the periods are equal and there is no obstacle to bringing help . . . And do not feel sorry for your property, for you will eat of the best of the upper land [Galilee]; therefore, hurry and emigrate, for I will maintain you . . . Be courageous!"

Because it was obviously never intended for publication, the diary follows no particular chronology, but consists largely of random discourses in the first person, with brief introdutions by Caro giving the times, places, and circumstances of the *maggid's* appearances. Though the greatest number of manifestations came as personifications of the Mishnah, the *maggid* appeared on occasion in other guises:

"I am the Mother."

"I am the Mother who chastises."

"I am the *Matrona*."

"I am the redeeming angel."

"I am the emissary of the Holy One, blessed be He . . . I watch over you steadily . . . The *Shekhinah* talks to you . . . You have attained what no one in a generation, during many preceding generations, succeeded in attaining."

The *maggid* taught Caro how to invoke it at will:

"Go to a pure place, thinking constantly of Torah without letting your thoughts wander even for a second, even while you are eating or talking. You must unify your limbs, body,

and soul in constant service to me, thinking of no other thing.
This is certainly true during the time for prayer. Nullify all
thoughts that enter your mind, for they are manifestations of
the ego . . .

"*Unify your heart constantly, at all times, at all hours, in all*
places, thinking of nothing except me, as I appear in my Torah
and ritual. This is the mystery of unity, where a person yokes
himself literally with his Creator. For the soul that attaches it-
self to Him, along with its body and limbs, literally becomes a
'*Camp of the Shekhinah.' This is what the Torah means when*
it says, 'You shall fear the Lord your God, serve Him, and
cleave to Him . . .' Your attitude toward everything in this
world must be one of detachment, for if one does not equate
the good of this world with its evil, he is not unifying himself
with his source completely."

For a sixteenth-century Kabbalist rooted in contemplation
of the spheres, it was quite natural for the *maggid* to reveal itself as the *Shekhinah*, the Mother, or God's immanent presence embodied in the sphere of *Sovereignty* and in the hidden
wisdom of the written Torah. Appearing as the Mishnah, the
maggid represented the oral Torah, embodied in the sphere of
Beauty. Caro probably recited the Mishnah as a chant with no
emphasis on its intellectual content, an exercise popular with
Kabbalists like his contemporary Rabbi Isaiah Hurwitz, who
wrote: "Happy is he who comes to know the six orders of the
Mishnah by heart, for thereby he makes a ladder on which his
soul ascends to the highest degree." In fact, Caro's mystical
contemporaries frequently joined "brotherhoods" which met
primarily to learn and recite the Mishnah by heart for the
purpose of inducing ecstasy. "If your eye could only be permitted to see, you would find yourself encompassed by troops
from every side. Some of them were created by the breath
that comes out from your mouth when you study the Mishnah," asserted the *maggid*.

Studying the chapters of the Mishnah that began with the
consonants spelling out the name of a departed relative, the
Kabbalist could ease that relative's spirit. For example, by re-

citing seven chapters of the treatise called "Niddah," which opens with the letter *D*, and Chapter 21 in the treatise called "Sabbath," which opens with the letter *N*, he commemorated the spirit of a man named *Dan*. There were even special handbooks citing mishnaic chapters and their opening letters in alphabetical order for this purpose.

To his mishnaic contemplation Caro added the recitation of the *Shema*, perhaps accompanied by the various breathing techniques outlined in the writings of fellow Kabbalist Chayim Vital. For the *maggid* had advised him to burn away all worldly thoughts "in the straw fire of your breath as you recite the *Shema*." Of the *maggid*'s 135 dated visitations, 109 took place on Friday evenings. It is said among Jewish mystics that an *ibbur*, or "additional soul," is loaned to all observers of the Sabbath. Perhaps this shared belief acted as a spur for Caro's more concentrated evocations. Eventually he grew so confident of the *maggid*'s appearance that he dropped the Mishnah recitation. This did not stop the voice from sounding of its own accord, addressing Caro as a *tzaddik*, and informing him that he had reached such high levels of *devekuth* as to no longer require contemplative formulas. Lavishing praises on him, the *maggid* addressed the new saint: "Whenever you go out into the street, my seven worlds and all their hosts escort you and proclaim before you, 'Pay homage to the holy image of the King! . . . Make place for the holy image of the King!" This meant that Caro had to be even more scrupulous in his behavior. "You must not sever your attachment to the Blessed Name for a single instance; for should you do it, the *Shekhinah* will fall down. And woe be to the man and to his fate who causes the destruction of all the worlds."

Again, it is important to remember how inextricably linked was the Jewish mystic with his many worlds. Kabbalists like Abraham Abulafia and Solomon Molko based their visions entirely on the messianic impulse, which carries with it the awesome responsibility of redemption. Thus, it was no empty admonition when the *maggid* warned Caro not to deflect his attention for even an instant. Any interruption would be a calamity, depriving not only Caro himself, but the entire cosmos, of the chance to reunite with the Source. Every Jewish mystic from the Middle Ages on in some way saw himself as a Messiah, Caro included. Confirmed as a *tzaddik*, he could plunge into still deeper states of *devekuth*. Now if he should so much as utter one word of the Mishnah with *kavanna* (one-pointed concentration), the *maggid* promised him, he would reach higher consciousness in an instant. Until this time, it said, Caro had been surrounded by only the first five lighted spheres from the lower part of the tree as he walked through the streets of Safed. But after having perfectly completed the Mishnah recitation, he was surrounded by six radiant lights, the new one being the divine attribute of *Beauty*.

Perhaps to refrain from pride and isolation from his fellows, Caro convinced himself that his slightest personal failing would bring about the failure of all mankind. So great, then, was the responsibility for a man of his communal interests that he simply could not permit himself to fail. Over and over again, the *maggid* stressed his frailty; even at the new peak of sanctity it could say, "If you only knew how many worlds suffer loss on account of your ceasing to meditate over the items of the law, you would have preferred death to life." So he plied himself with further concentration exercises, imagining the Tetragrammaton always suspended before his eyes inscribed in black ink on a piece of white parchment; walking along the road distributing Torah thoughts in time with each step; thinking incessantly of the Mishnah, the Torah, and the Tetragrammaton even as he ate, drank, or talked. Increasingly devoting himself to ascetic disciplines, Caro took food without spice and allowed himself only one glass of water at night. The *maggid*, too, seemed intent on mortifying him: "During the day you should not drink at all." He embarked on forty-day fasts to commemorate the forty-day development of the embryo into recognizably human form and, analogously, the spiritual rebirth he was undergoing by means of self-purification. Now so intent on abstaining from all pleasurable foods, he was admonished by the *maggid* in frequently comical dialogues: "How can you wish me to talk to you after you have eaten horseradish?" asked the offended *maggid.* "I have already hinted to you on the mystery of the good over the bad odors." For a Kabbalist like Caro, spicy food stimulated the animal soul and therefore bound him even further to temporal desires.

THE HIGHEST VISION

Once Caro had mastered control of even his apparently harmless remaining appetites, he could evoke the highest vision, that of Elijah himself. As the *maggid* put it:

> He shall talk to you mouth to mouth and greet you, for he will be your guide and master in order to teach you all the mysteries of the Torah . . . Elijah clothes himself in a body to be visible in this world. And whenever you wish that he become visible to you, concentrate [on him] at bedtime. There are three ways of seeing him: in a dream . . . while awake and greeting him . . . while awake, greeting him, and being greeted in return. You will be raised to the third degree. You will see him while awake, greet him, and be greeted by him in return; but he will appear to you when you do not expect him.

After fasting for three days and nights for seven weeks running and seated alone in his meditation chamber, Caro successfully evoked the prophet. Elijah, dressed in white, entered the room, sat down opposite him, and began "conversing" with Joseph Caro face to face.

Perfect *devekuth* results only from perfect meditation. When the Jewish mystic practiced withdrawal of thought, first from the external world and then from the world of thought itself, he was "bound in the bundle of life"—that is, he attained both fearlessness in the face of death and immortality. It was no longer, therefore, Joseph Caro, or Isaac Luria, or Abraham Abulafia, or Nehuniah ben Hakana who spoke, or willed, or acted, but the *Shekhinah* herself, working through them. The Jew, having reached the state called *devekuth,* saw himself as nothing more than a vehicle for "universal truth." His *devekuth* afforded him complete indifference to pleasure and pain alike; his life was devoted to service from which he, as an independent personality, was totally detached. The fruits of his labors were entirely sacrificed to the needs of his fellow creatures.

Liberated by his penetration of life's paradoxes, the mystic "saw" God against the clear mirror of his own soul. By practicing *hitbodedut,* meditation in a secluded place within himself, he yoked himself to heaven, developing a power of love so great that it literally drew down the divine influx into his body.

Moses, the greatest Jewish spiritual master, had obtained the perfect *devekuth.* Yet he remained whole, alert, calm. All this, Moses accomplished in the high place called Sinai which, sages have said, meant a state of meditation figuratively referred to as "Sinai," as well as an actual mountain. Even the prophet's own sons could not assume the teaching; only Joshua, who "did not depart" from Moses' side, remaining in perfect *hitbodedut* with him from his boyhood, could absorb the "tradition," and pass it on to the generations which followed. These teachings, practiced in seclusion, come down to us as *Kabbalah.* Combining contemplation, sensory deprivation, chanting, and ritual worship, the key to the tradition was *kavanna,* a form of one-pointed concentration which also signified pure devotion.

With his body freed from worldly attachment, his mind cut off from its ruminations and his heart set on God, the Kabbalist pronounced the sacred Name. When the sense of the words had disappeared entirely, when the devotee no longer could define where he began and his "prayer" ended, he had reached *devekuth*. Like Moses, who had marshaled the Children of Israel into camps, the Kabbalist marshaled all his faculties and visualized any one of a number of great moments in the history of his people: the community of Israel gathered at Mount Sinai; Abraham and Isaac at Mount Moriah; the Temple service performed by the High Priest. Inscribing these scenes in all their splendor on his mind's eye, he rose to inaugurate the daily prayers with true *kavanna*.

"Such hours of prayer," said medieval poet and mystic Yehudah Ha-Levi, "[are] the heart and fruit of his time, the rest of his time being like so many paths leading up to it . . . for then he resembles the most spiritual beings and is farthest removed from animality." Prayer with *kavanna*, according to Maimonides, meant standing directly in the presence of the *Shekhinah*. Even the singing of a peddler outside his window reminded the mystic of God; thus incorporated into his prayer, that simple song could sweep him into *devekuth*.

The Jewish mystical path is long, arduous, austere, joyous, isolated and communal, ethereal and earthy all at once. For two thousand years it was plagued by charlatanism from within and hostility from without; in modern times it has virtually disappeared. But as we approach the twenty-first century of the Common Era—if the 1930s predictions of the late Kabbalist Rabbi Abraham Isaac Kook are right—Jewish mysticism may well surface again.

EPILOGUE
Personal Musings on a Future Kabbalah

Ours is an age of jet-borne gurus. On any plane going to and
from India you see them, orange-robed, surrounded by wor-
shipful American disciples—60 per cent of whom, statistics
tell us, are Jewish. For Jewish mysticism has become a museum piece, an interesting if grotesque offshoot from the normative Jewish tree. People are willing to study it, to speculate
about it, even a few rabbis can be goaded into explaining it
away, but nobody really practices it—at least, not in the way
it has been described in the preceding pages. Once, at a Har-
vard lecture, I heard a rabbi tell a student who had asked a
question about the *Zohar:* "Well, that's not Judaism; it's mysticism." So it isn't surprising to find planeloads of Cohens and
Schwartzes with shaven heads and rings in their nostrils
headed for the message directly from the "spiritual" East. Judaism is, after all, preoccupied with *this* world, of which the
new Buddhists and yogis have had their fill. Meditation has
led millions of Westerners into another dimension of psychic
experience—for some, another "high," more mystical even
than that produced by the hallucinogens of the sixties. Eastern mysticism offers, it would seem, a way out of the very
earthy, political drama which is the focus of the current Jewish experience. Go to Israel and ask a saintly rabbi with a reputation for mystical leanings to teach you the Abulafian letter
meditations, and he throws back his frail white head with a

Devekuth: Cleaving to God

"Chas ve chalilah!"—God forbid! Go to India and almost as soon as you have cleared customs you'll find someone ready to teach you the secrets of raising your *kundalini* (spiritual energy residing at the base of the spine).

On the other hand, a respectable number of young Jewish refugees from Zen have grown back their hair and exchanged the bald, clear, militant experience of "sitting" for the hairy Hasidic mode of Lubavitch. Discipline of one kind or another is "in"—even if it means keeping kosher and being entirely absorbed in ritual. It is not uncommon to find an occasional "new" Hasid wearing his old Hindu beads over his *tzizith*. Traditional Hasidim are welcoming back their "lost" Jewish souls with open arms and, in some cases, with a missionary zeal reminiscent of the Sun Myung Moonies. Why do the remnants of the Jewish mystical tradition want their children back? Is there an underground rumor that a new Baal Shem Tov is about to be incarnated as we usher in the twenty-first century of the Common Era? Perhaps that explains the sudden proliferation of "Aquarian" Hasidim, themselves experimenters with the exotic East, renegade rabbis who are incorporating the wisdom of all ages and traditions into the Kabbalah in preparation for the unified world to come. *The Jewish Catalog,* the latest repository for counterculture Judaism, would appear to be preparing the twenty-first-century Jewish mystic for a new Safed, perhaps in Maine, or the Pennsylvania farm country, where macrobiotic and other kosher vegetarians will dance in honor of the Sabbath Queen; perhaps gathered behind their female guru, herself decked in phylacteries and prayer shawl—if Jewish feminists have their way.

But even this "new age" amalgam of drug culture, Eastern mysticism, and radical politics has not yet been able to co-ordinate a practicable Jewish system comparable to the highly organized Zen, Yoga, and Sufi groups that are, ironically, moving into the old "borscht circuit" hotels in the Catskills recently vacated by Jews. Nor has anyone been able to clearly expound the practice of Kabbalah as, say, the Ari did for all degrees of disciples; or Rabbi Akiva; or Rabbi Simeon bar Yohai. No *Chaverim,* or Comrades, gather with the specific aim of achieving *devekuth.* What you find in the diehard leftovers of the tradition are rules for punctilious observation of the precepts, but without the instructions for *kavanna* that went into making them the exercise in mindfulness that is the basis for all mystical disciplines. Even those groups who pride themselves on being "different" from ordinary mainstream Jews still gather in Brooklyn to speculate about the possible meanings of the sayings of dead Jewish masters, their women dutifully baking bread in the kitchen. Sometimes there will be singing, but nobody, not even the most scholarly exponent, can claim a working knowledge of the Ari's *kavannot,* those mantralike meditation symbols that cover the daily prayer book like like a tantalizing, indecipherable code. Ask about it and you are told that the Ari's methods are "not for our age." And certainly not the mentally dangerous journeys of the *Merkabah.*

It's strange. You don't think of asking your Japanese Zen master to "adapt" his timeworn techniques for a new age. Instead you sit in an American Buddhist monastery on your knees and eat oatmeal with chopsticks because you are dutifully following the "tradition." Nor would any true Aquarian believe in a guru who exchanged his loincloth for a pinstriped banker's suit (one of the main reasons, I think, that the impeccably tailored Krishnamurti gathers followers who are mostly past forty). The meditation techniques presented to us by our jet-propelled swamis have not—except for the publicity-wise Maharishi—been recycled to fit the needs of the Western mind and body. Instead, their followers are asked to chant in languages they don't understand; to perform ceremonies honoring gods they have only experienced in picture books; and even, in some cases, to adopt the dress and food habits of a foreign clime and culture that does not befit their own immediate surroundings. Yet the Jewish mystic is constantly being

Devekuth: Cleaving to God

asked to "modernize," to throw out all the "irrelevant" para-phernalia like ritual baths, Sabbath, and prayer. Maybe that's why the prodigal sons and daughters are returning to Jewish ritual with such a vengeance. Why pray in someone else's language when, since your Bar Mitzvah, you haven't prayed in your own?

It isn't a question of modernizing, revamping, adapting, or returning at all, but rather of learning how to apply what Jews already have. The preparations and paths have been outlined in this book. They are as valid a form of spiritual training as any from the Far East. In fact, many of them might talk more intimately to the Western Jewish soul. I know a young woman who comfortably integrates her Indian meditation with her Hasidic ritual life. All kinds of interesting hybrids are possible. At the end of the training, sages tell us, there is no need for systems at all. Once you reach the top of the mountain, you can get off your donkey. Much of what passes for meditation, spiritual life, and discipline is nothing more than continuing to carry that donkey around on your back as if it were the true and visible mark of your "enlightenment"—whether it be a Jewish donkey, a Zen donkey, or a Yoga donkey.

For those who will be comfortable with it, the Kabbalah offers clear-cut instructions for achieving ecstatic states (Has-idism); rational, self-investigative meditation (Lurianic Kabbalah); concentration and visualization techniques (Abulafian *tzeruf*); and psychological insight meditation (*Merkabah*). The wrappings may appear exotic; the Bible as taught in Sunday school has inhibited a whole generation of potential Jewish mystics. Who wouldn't keep away from a jealous, exclusively masculine God intent on killing off everybody in His path? Yet you have merely to glimpse into the *Zohar* to open a whole new and glorious vision of the formidable world of Yahweh.

What about the teachers? If you are so blessed, you may, on first sitting, elicit a *maggid* or Elijah himself. Then you will

161

have found the ideal spiritual master—the inner guru. Most of us are not quite that elevated. For the ordinary incipient Kabbalist it would be better to begin by reading some of the original materials—best, in Hebrew, second best, in translation. The words of the teachers themselves are the most potent, they still ring through the pages in their original voices. One learned Kabbalist I know practices according to the teachings of a medieval master whose manuscript has become his "living" guide. Bahya Ibn Paquda's advice on preparation in everyday life is still the foundation for further practice. One need not be traditionally "religious" to perform this rigorous self-observation technique. It is an indispensable prerequisite to any contemplation—especially the Abulafian kind which, because of its psychic intensity, may damage an unstable mind or body.

Today there are no actively recruiting Kabbalists—no posters on college campuses announcing intensive meditation sessions, no encounters, only every now and then a scholarly Kabbalist who might drop a hint or two in a lecture on Jewish mysticism. If you already meditate, try substituting the *Shema* as a focus for concentration, or one of the "scenes" suggested by Rabbi Simeon bar Yohai for visualization: the gathering of Israel at Sinai, picturing your own limbs and thoughts being marshaled toward that central place. A trip to Israel is helpful, but not required; the Kabbalah, being portable, has accompanied the Jews throughout their two-thousand-year exile and is just as valid when studied in New Jersey as in Jerusalem. However, the Sephardic tradition—the most poetic by far—can best be understood when practiced in Israel. Middle Eastern and North African rabbis living there have no inhibitions about calling themselves Kabbalists or mystics. You have only to approach them in their houses, in their *yeshivoth*, or on their receiving days. The only barriers there will be language and cultural foreignness. Note, however, that those Westerners who have really committed themselves to Tibetan Buddhism, for example, have learned to read the sutras in

Devekuth: Cleaving to God

Tibetan, and that those who study Vedanta in a traditional Indian ashram study Sanskrit and sit in separately designated sections for men and women. Cultural padding and ornamentation is the most annoying part—for a freewheeling, individualistic American—of any meditative discipline. Attempts have been made by many to distill the essential experience from the religious trappings, but, to my knowledge, no one has succeeded fully. Ritual of one sort or another, I suppose, is an inevitable hurdle in the "donkey" part of the journey.

Because Kabbalists as a rule talk rather than write, it is impossible to locate the ideal master of the "tradition" from current books. There are no "universities of Kabbalah" experimenting on the physical effects of *tzeruf*, no intellectual centers for Kabbalists to gather in and exchange ideas on the "new" Kabbalah. There is no *new* Kabbalah. Only an old one, which nobody in the twentieth century has improved on—yet. Most easily found are the Hasidic centers which, if you wade through the traditional orthodoxy, can give a glimmer of the spark within. The wading, unfortunately, too often takes a lifetime. Some of the Hasidic techniques are best learned from much publicized liberal rabbis like Zalman Schachter, leader of the *Bnai Or* (Children of Light) Congregation in Philadelphia. Kabbalists of various stripes, I am told, inhabit every major city in Israel, most of them so quietly that only the undaunted seeker can locate them. No real teacher of Kabbalah will advertise; if you are lucky, you'll hear of him or her by word of mouth. Like Larry Darrell in Somerset Maugham's *The Razor's Edge,* you just have to go on looking for yourself.

GLOSSARY

Adam Kadmon   metaphorical "body of God."

Aravot   a sacred place inhabited by the departed souls of saints and sages.

Bahir   "Book of Light," eleventh-century French mystic's handbook.

Binah   the sphere of *Understanding* on the cosmic tree.

Bittul ha-yesh   annihilation of the desiring self, or ego.

Chaverim   "Comrades," a group of mystics in sixteenth-century Safed.

Chayot   "lightning flash" vision described by Ezekiel, symbol of a highly ecstatic state among *Merkabah* mystics.

Cheshek   mystic enthusiasm.

Daath   the secret sphere of *Knowledge* on the cosmic tree.

Devekuth   the state of cleaving to God.

Dillug   "skipping," a meditative exercise in free association of ideas according to specific code words.

Dodi   "dear friend," the stage at which the mystic is bound to God by Love rather than Awe.

Elohim Hayim   "the living God," a state of ecstatic consciousness achieved by deep concentration.

En Sof   the Infinite.

Etrog   citron fruit, visualized at the core of the heart during meditation.

Gilgulim   incarnations.

Glossary

Hakhanot Hasidic preparations for prayer: meditation, ritual washing, dressing in non-woolen garments.

Halakha Jewish legal tradition.

Haluk garment of light surrounding God's glory visible to *Merkabah* mystics.

Hasagah Lubavitcher Hasidic emphasis on intellect as the way to God.

Hasid mystic devotee.

Hasiduth devotion to God.

Hebel breath, connected with meditative breathing exercises using the text of Ecclesiastes.

Hekhalot halls of God's palace.

Histapkut "making do," the ascetic attitude of the medieval school of Isaac of Akko.

Hitbodedut meditation.

Hitlahavut Hasidic enthusiasm.

Hitpaalut Hasidic rapture following contemplative prayer.

Hokhmah the sphere of *Wisdom* on the cosmic tree.

Ibbur the additional soul lent to all Sabbath observers on that day.

Kabbalah over-all title for Jewish mystical tradition.

Kavanna one-pointed concentration.

Kavannot symbols in Lurianic prayer book to induce one-pointed concentration.

Kisupha yearning for the Divine.

Lulav palm branch, symbolic of the human spine in meditative visualization.

Madregot levels of mystic ascent.

Maggid a preacher in ordinary life; a celestial guardian in spiritual life.

Maskil enlightened.

Matrona the female aspect of God; also called *Shekhinah*.

Mechavenim those who make prayers with meditation.

Merkabah Throne mysticism, prevalent in the first two centuries of the Common Era; also defined as "chariot," "combining," and "grafting" by mystics who permutated Hebrew letters.

Mishnah oral law compiled in third century c.e. by Judah the Prince.

Mitzvah divine precept.

Mohin degadlut expanded consciousness achieved in Hasidic ecstasy.

Neshamah spiritual portion of the soul.

Niggun wordless melody used to induce meditative states among Lubavitcher Hasidim.

Ofanim wheel-shaped angelic beings.

Pardes the "garden" symbolizing Jewish mystical practice.

Rav master.

Rav Ha-Hasid master of devotion.

Rebbe Hasidic master.

Sefer Yetzirah first-century mystic handbook for permutating God's Names.

Shedim demonic beings who confuse the mind in meditation.

Shefa divine influx.

Shekhinah God's female aspect and immanent presence, also called *Matrona;* resides in the sphere of *Sovereignty* on the cosmic tree.

Shema daily recitation of God's oneness.

Shem Hameforesh the Specific Name of God.

Tannaitic period of Jewish history devoted to compilation of oral law c.e. 1–5).

Tetragrammaton YHVH, sacred Name of God.

Tevunah a Hasidic stage in contemplation where subject-object separation disappears.

Tikkun spiritual "correction" exercise.

Tzaddik enlightened saint.

Tzeruf mental Hebrew letter permutation.

Tzizith fringes worn by men outside their clothing to observe the biblical commandment in Numbers 15:37–41.

Yechidah union with the Absolute.

Yichud mental "binding" exercise initiated by Isaac Luria, the Ari of Safed.

Zohar "Book of Splendor," a thirteenth-century Spanish mystic's guide, central to Kabbalism from medieval times.

BIBLIOGRAPHY

Primary Sources

Abarbanel, Isaac. "Nachalot Avot." Commentary on *Sayings of the Fathers*. Venice, 1545. Trans. Aryeh Kaplan. New York, 1953.

Abulafia, Abraham. *Ve-Zot Le-Yehudah.* Quoted in A. Jellinek, *Ginzay Hokhmot Na-Kabbalah.* Leipzig, 1853, pp. 13ff. Trans. Aryeh Kaplan.

———. *Sheva Netivot Ha-Torah.* Quoted in A. Jellinek, *Philosophie und Kabbalah.* Leipzig, 1854. Trans. Aryeh Kaplan.

———. *Otzer Eden Ganuz.* Bodleian MS. Or.606. Trans. Aryeh Kaplan.

———. *Sefer Ha-Tzeruf.* Bibliothèque National MS. ※774 and Jewish Theological Seminary MS. ※1887. Trans. Aryeh Kaplan.

———. *Mafteach Ha-Hokhmoth.* Jewish Theological Seminary MS. ※1686. Trans. Aryeh Kaplan.

———. *Mafteach Ha-Shemoth.* Jewish Theological Seminary MS. ※1897. Trans. Aryeh Kaplan.

———. *Or Ha-Sechel.* Vatican MS. ※233. Trans. Aryeh Kaplan.

———. *Sefer Ha-Cheshek.* Jewish Theological Seminary MS. ※858. Trans. Aryeh Kaplan.

——. *Chayey Olam Habah.* Hebrew University MS. ✡8°540. Trans. Aryeh Kaplan.

Albotini, Yehuda. *Sulam Ha-Aliyah.* Hebrew University MSS. ✡334 and ✡1302. Trans. Aryeh Kaplan.

Bahya Ibn Paquda. *The Book of Direction to the Duties of the Heart.* Trans. Menahem Mansoor. London: Routledge and Kegan Paul, 1973.

Caro, Joseph. *Maggid Mesharim.* Lublin, 1551 ed. Selections trans. Aryeh Kaplan.

Charles, R. H., ed. and trans. *The Book of Enoch.* London: S.P.C.K., 1962.

Cordovero, Moses. *The Palm Tree of Deborah.* Trans. Louis Jacobs. New York: Hermon Press, 1974.

——. *Pardes Rimonim.* Venice, 1586. Trans. Aryeh Kaplan.

——. *Sefer Or Yakar.* Quoted in G. Scholem, *Kitvey Yad Ba-Kabbalah.* Jerusalem: Hebrew University Press, 1930, p. 232. Trans. Aryeh Kaplan.

Dov Baer of Lubavitch. *Tract on Ecstasy.* Trans. Louis Jacobs. London: Vallentine Mitchell, 1963.

Isaac of Akko. *Otzer Ha-Chayim.* Hebrew University MS. ✡775–✡1062. Trans. Aryeh Kaplan.

Luzzatto, Moses Chayim. *Derech Ha-Shem.* Trans. Aryeh Kaplan. New York: Feldheim, forthcoming.

——. *The Path of the Just.* Trans. Shraga Silverstein. Jerusalem: Feldheim, 1974.

Maimonides, Abraham. *Sefer Ha-Maspik Leovdey Ha-Shem.* Trans. from Arabic to Hebrew by Yosef ben Tzalach Dori; trans. from Hebrew to English by Aryeh Kaplan. Jerusalem, 1965.

Maimonides, Moses. "Thirteen Principles of Faith." In *Maimonides' Principles.* 2d ed. Trans., with additions, Aryeh Kaplan. New York: National Conference of Synagogue Youth, 1975.

Sefer Bahir. Trans. Aryeh Kaplan. New York: Samuel Weiser, forthcoming.

"Selections from Hekhalot Rabatai." Trans. Aryeh Kaplan, in

his *Meditation and Kabbalah.* New York: Samuel Weiser, forthcoming.

"Selections from Pirkey Hekhalot." Trans. Aryeh Kaplan. Unpublished MS.

Shem Tov the Sephardi. *Shaarey Tzedek.* Columbia University MS. ※X893, ※Sh43. Trans. Aryeh Kaplan.

Tzayach, Joseph ben Abraham Ibn. *Even Ha-Shoham* and *Sherit Yosef.* Hebrew University MSS. ※8⁰416. Trans. Aryeh Kaplan.

Uzieli, Chayim Yosef David. *Midbar Kadmut.* Lvov, 1870. Trans. Aryeh Kaplan.

Vital, Chayim. *Shaarey Kedushah.* Constantinople, 1731. Trans. Aryeh Kaplan.

——. *Shaarey Kedushah, Pt. IV.* British Museum MS ※749. Trans. Aryeh Kaplan.

——. "Shaarey Ruach Ha-Kodesh." Selections trans. Aryeh Kaplan, in his *Meditation and Kabbalah.* New York: Samuel Weiser, forthcoming.

Zohar. Vols. 1–5. Trans. H. Sperling and M. Simon. London: Soncino Press, 1933.

Secondary Sources

Abelson, J. *Jewish Mysticism.* New York: Hermon Press, 1969.

Bension, Ariel. *The Zohar in Moslem and Christian Spain.* New York: Hermon Press, 1932.

Chang Chung-yuan. *Creativity and Taoism.* New York: Harper & Row, 1970.

Enelow, H. G. "Kawwana: The Struggle for Inwardness in Judaism." In *Studies in Jewish Literature.* Berlin: Georg Reimer, 1913.

Fluegel, Maurice. *Philosophy, Qabbala and Vedanta.* Baltimore: H. Fluegel, 1902.

Ginzburg, Simon. *The Life and Works of Moses Hayyim Luzzatto.* Philadelphia: Dropsie College Press, 1931.

Hurwitz, Siegmund. "Psychological Aspects in Early Hasidic

Bibliography

Literature." In *Timeless Documents of the Soul.* Evanston, Ill.: Northwestern University Press, 1968.

Jacobs, Louis. *Hasidic Prayer.* London: Routledge & Kegan Paul, 1972.

Kaplan, Aryeh. "Sparks in the Night." Unpublished MS.

———. "The Light Beyond: Adventures in Hasidic Thought." Unpublished MS.

———. *Meditation and Kabbalah.* New York: Samuel Weiser, forthcoming.

———. *Rabbi Nachman's Wisdom.* New York: Hermon Press, 1973.

Mindel, Nissan. *Rabbi Schneur Zalman of Liadi.* 2 vols. New York: Kehot Publication Society, 1973.

Rabinowicz, Harry M. *The World of Hasidism.* Hartford, Conn.: Hartmore House, 1970.

Rosenberg, Roy A. *The Anatomy of God.* New York: Ktav Publishing House, 1973.

Rubinstein, Aryeh. *Hasidism.* New York and Paris: Leon Amiel, 1975.

Schechter, Solomon. "Safed in the Sixteenth Century." In *Studies in Judaism.* 2d series. Philadelphia: Jewish Publication Society, 1945.

Scholem, Gershom. "Ha-Kabbalah Shel Sefer Ha-Temunah ve Shel A. Abulafia." In *Perakim Betoldot Ha-Kabbalah Besefard,* No. 2. Ed. Dr. Y. ben Shlomo. Jerusalem, 1965.

———. *Jewish Gnosticism, Merkabah Mysticism, and Talmudic Tradition.* 2d ed. New York: Jewish Theological Seminary Press, 1965.

———. *Major Trends in Jewish Mysticism.* New York: Schocken, 1961.

Staal, Frits. *Exploring Mysticism.* Berkeley: University of California Press, 1975.

Werblowsky, Zvi. *Joseph Caro, Lawyer and Mystic.* New York: Oxford University Press, 1962.

Zwelling, Jeremy. "Androgynous God, Androgynous Man: A Kabbalistic Interpretation." Unpublished MS.

~~Field of Dreams~~ (video)

Friendships Field 94 minutes

1-800-347-2833